Master Bits & Mercenary Bites

GIRLS NIGHT

MASTER *Bits &* MERCENARY *Bites*

GIRLS NIGHT

SHORT STORIES & SLICES OF LIFE BY
NEW YORK TIMES BESTSELLING AUTHOR
LEXI BLAKE

RECIPES FROM USA TODAY BESTSELLING AUTHOR
SUZANNE M. JOHNSON

EVIL EYE
CONCEPTS

Master Bits & Mercenary Bites

Girls Night Copyright 2017 DLZ Entertainment LLC
Recipes Copyright 2017 Suzanne McCollum Johnson

ISBN: 978-1-948050-05-0

Published by Evil Eye Concepts, Incorporated

All rights reserved. No part of this book may be reproduced, scanned, or distributed in any printed or electronic form without permission. Please do not participate in or encourage piracy of copyrighted materials in violation of the author's rights.

This is a work of fiction. Names, places, characters and incidents are the product of the author's imagination and are fictitious. Any resemblance to actual persons, living or dead, events or establishments is solely coincidental.

Introduction

Girls Night is my second collaboration with the fabulous Suzanne Johnson, my friend and home cooking expert. Why try this again? Well, we had so much fun the first time and there's so much more Suzanne has to teach us all about making life delicious. But beyond the food and fun, I realized that these characters of mine don't stop talking to me simply because the book ends. For me, these characters have breath and meaning that lasts long after the final page is turned.

I decided I wanted to concentrate on the women of McKay-Taggart this time so you'll find a lot of easy prep meals. Suzanne will show you how to use a crock pot and what's in your cupboard to make a meal to please everyone—because like the women of MT, we're working women and stay-at-home moms, harried daughters and women on the move, but we all have someone to take care of and so often the way we show our love is in the kitchen.

These stories are about how we stay together long after the happily ever after, how we support and love each other. You'll find some of your favorite couples coping with everyday struggles and leaning on each other.

And one writer will find her way back to a place she worried she would never go again. One writer will discover that what seemed lost can be found again, and the road to home, though long and winding, sometimes leads to Bliss.

My goal with this book is to make you laugh and cry, to share some amazing recipes because like food, stories should bring us all together. So I invite you to my table where Charlotte and Serena and the rest of the women will welcome you with a glass of wine and embrace you like family.

I hope you'll see yourself in some of these stories. They were written for you.

Love,

Lexi

Table of Contents

Chapter 1 - Charlotte

Bacon Wrapped Shrimp 2
Stuffed Mushrooms 3
Coconut Shrimp 4
Bacon Ranch Cheese Ball 5
Beef Wellington 6
Slice of Life - Phoebe and Jesse in "Mischief Managed" 7
Slow Cooker Pork Tenderloin with Pineapple 18
Slow Cooker Beef and Broccoli 19
Chocolate Cake with Chocolate Icing 20
Strawberry Pretzel Salad 21
Sparkling Screwdriver 22
Charlotte and Ian's story - Rough Night 23

Chapter 2 - Faith

Slow Cooker Spinach & Artichoke Dip 46
Cheesy Monkey Bread 47
Meatball Sliders 48
Sausage Ravioli Alfredo 49
Slice of Life - Karina and Derek in "Stakeout Takeout" 50
Slow Cooker Stuffed Bell Peppers 60
Slow Cooker Pizza Chicken 61
Artichoke Salad 62
Easy Tiramisu 63
Faith and Ten's story - Unexpected Gifts 64

Chapter 3 - Serena

Texas Caviar 82

Taco Ring of Fire 83

Burrito Love 84

Southwest Chicken 85

Slow Cooker Cheeseburger Meatloaf 86

Slice of Life - Tiffany and Sebastian in "After Hours" 87

Slow Cooker Chili 95

Stuffed French Toast 96

Apple Turnovers 97

Ice Cream Cake 98

Blackberry Moscow Mule... 99

Serena's story - Broke Down in Bliss 100

Chapter 4 - Penny

Hot Ham & Cheese Rolls 128

Wild Rice Dressing with Sausage & Cranberries 129

Slow Cooker Chicken & Dumplings 130

Slow Cooker Honey Soy Pot Roast 131

Easy Breakfast Casserole 132

Slice of Life - Damon and Penny in "She's the Boss" 133

Banana Pudding 145

Peach Cobbler 146

Key Lime Cake 147

Spiked Strawberry Lemonade 148

Women of McKay-Taggart - The Long Wait 149

Bacon Wrapped Shrimp
Stuffed Mushrooms
Coconut Shrimp
Bacon Ranch Cheese Ball
Beef Wellington
Slow Cooker Pork Tenderloin with Pineapple
Slow Cooker Beef and Broccoli
Chocolate Cake with Chocolate Icing
Strawberry Pretzel Salad
Sparkling Screwdriver

Slice of Life

Phoebe and Jesse in
"Mischief Managed"

Charlotte and Ian's story

Rough Night

Bacon Wrapped Shrimp

¼ cup brown sugar

¼ cup soy sauce

Juice of 1 lemon

24 large shrimp

8 slices bacon

Preheat oven to 425 degrees. Mix together the brown sugar, soy sauce and lemon juice in a small bowl and pour into a resealable bag. Add shrimp to the bag and toss to coat. Refrigerate shrimp for 30 minutes. While the shrimp are marinating, cut bacon slices into thirds. Wrap 1/3 slice of bacon around each shrimp and place seam side down on a greased cookie sheet. Bake for 10-12 minutes.

Stuffed Mushrooms

1 POUND GROUND SAUSAGE

1 (8 OUNCE) PACKAGE CREAM CHEESE

2 (4 OUNCE) PACKAGES FRESH BUTTON MUSHROOMS, STEMS REMOVED

CHIVES, CHOPPED (OPTIONAL)

Preheat oven to 450 degrees. In a large skillet, cook sausage over medium heat until browned. Drain, add to a medium size bowl and mix with cream cheese. Stuff mushroom caps with sausage mixture and place in a 9 x 13-inch baking dish. Bake for 8-10 minutes. Garnish with chives, if desired.

Coconut Shrimp

OIL FOR FRYING (ABOUT 4-6 CUPS)

2 CUPS PANKO BREADCRUMBS

1 CUP SWEETENED COCONUT

1 CUP MILK

1 EGG

2 TABLESPOONS ALL-PURPOSE FLOUR

SALT AND PEPPER TO TASTE

1 POUND (21-30 COUNT) RAW SHRIMP, PEELED AND DEVEINED

In a deep fryer, bring oil to 350 degrees. Mix together the panko breadcrumbs and coconut in a medium bowl. In a separate bowl, mix together the milk, egg and flour. Salt and pepper the shrimp and dip in the milk mixture and then dredge in the panko/coconut mixture. Drop the shrimp about 4 at a time into the oil and fry for 3-5 minutes or until golden brown. Drain on paper towels and serve with the soy marmalade sauce (recipe below).

Soy Marmalade Sauce

1 CUP ORANGE MARMALADE

¼ CUP SOY SAUCE

Combine the marmalade and soy sauce in a small saucepan and bring to a simmer over low heat. Simmer for 3-5 minutes. Remove from heat.

Bacon Ranch Cheese Ball

2 (8 ounce) packages cream cheese

1 tablespoon ranch dressing mix

½ cup sharp cheddar cheese, shredded

½ cup real bacon bits

¼ cup green onion, chopped

1 cup pecans, chopped

Combine the first 5 ingredients. When blended, form into a ball and roll in chopped pecans to cover. Serve with crackers.

Beef Wellington

2 TABLESPOONS BUTTER

1/4 POUND FRESH MUSHROOMS, FINELY CHOPPED

1 GARLIC CLOVE, MINCED

1/4 TEASPOON DRIED THYME

1 (17.3 OUNCE) PACKAGE FROZEN PUFF PASTRY DOUGH, THAWED

4 (4-5 OUNCE) BEEF TENDERLOIN STEAKS, 1-INCH THICK

SALT AND PEPPER TO TASTE

¼ CUP DIJON MUSTARD

1 EGG

Preheat oven to 425 degrees. In a small skillet over medium heat, melt butter and sauté mushrooms, garlic, and thyme 6-8 minutes, or until mushrooms are tender. Remove from heat and set aside. Unfold puff pastry sheets and cut each in half crosswise. Spoon mushroom mixture onto center of each of the 4 pieces of puff pastry, distributing evenly. Season both sides of tenderloin steaks with salt and pepper and rub evenly with Dijon mustard. Place over mushroom mixture. Bring corners of pastry up over steaks; using your fingers, pinch corners and edges together to seal completely. Place seam-side down on baking sheet. Whisk together egg and 2 tablespoons of water to make egg wash. Brush evenly over each puff pastry and bake 20-25 minutes. Steaks will be medium rare.

Slice of Life

Phoebe and Jesse in "Mischief Managed"

Phoebe Murdoch looked up from her computer as Jake and Adam stood in her doorway. "I'm sorry, what did you say?"

The two men crowded inside. Tristan held Adam's hand while Jake cradled their daughter in his arms. Both men looked completely harried.

"Serena's car broke down and then some asshole arrested her, but only because his wife is a huge fan and now they're going to Misery her. I just know it," Adam said, his voice breathless.

"I don't want them to Misery my momma," Tristan said, his eyes wide with tears.

Jake sent Adam a look that could have frozen fire. "Don't be such a dramatic idiot. I talked to her. She's fine. Tris, buddy, Mommy's perfectly fine. I talked to a very nice lady named Nell who thinks it would be nice for Daddy and Papa to go spend a day with Mommy and then bring her home."

Jesse stepped up, leaning against the doorway. His long, lean body caught her eye, but then it always did. Her husband had the single brightest smile she'd ever seen, and it never failed to make her day better. "So you've come begging for babysitting? Is that why Big Tag ran out of here like his freaking pants were on fire?"

She'd heard Ian had surprise plans for Charlotte tonight. Big Tag would definitely try to avoid anything that would put their date night in jeopardy. She was amazed he hadn't asked her to watch their monsters. They got along well with Jamie. He'd probably asked Alex and Eve. And it was a good thing because apparently they were taking in the Dean-Miles kiddos.

"I suspect so," she said. There was something playing around in the back of her mind. Some illusive thought that she couldn't quite catch. It had plagued her all day. She'd started the stuffed bell peppers in the slow cooker this morning and tried to figure out what she was missing. She'd even gone over the ingredients three times to make sure she hadn't left one out. It had to be something else. Or it was absolutely nothing, since she hadn't caught it all damn day. "So you're asking us if we can watch Brianna and Tris while you run away to Colorado to save Serena from some crazy fans?"

"I believe they are," Jesse said, winking her way.

Damn that man was hot. How long had it been since they threw down? Too long. Jamie was a handful. She adored their son, but parenthood played hell on more babymaking. Still, they wouldn't turn down their friends. "We left Jamie with a sitter because he said he didn't feel well this morning, but she says he hasn't run a fever and he's seemed fine all day. If you're okay with that, of course, we can keep them. Do they have all their things?"

Jake took that moment to bundle Brianna into Jesse's arms. "Excellent. We have to go home and pack quickly. I'll drop off some clothes for tomorrow on our way to the airport."

"I don't know why we have to pack," Adam said. "According to the crazy lady, they're holding Serena at a nudist resort."

"What's a nudist?" Tristan asked.

Jake frowned his partner's way. "You get that one."

Adam sighed and dropped to one knee, looking his son in the face. "It's nothing to worry about, Tris. Like Daddy said, Mommy's taking a little break, but we'll bring her back very soon and it's going to be okay."

Jake leaned over and kissed Brianna before picking Tristan up for a hug. "Love you, son. And seriously, your mom is fine. I just talked to her and she's better than she's been in months. She's good, buddy. And I'm going to bring you back something cool."

Tristan's eyes lit up. "Okay, Daddy."

When Jake straightened up, he shook his head Adam's way but said nothing.

Adam looked a bit sheepish. "Sorry. I freaked out a little. It's not every day I find out my wife has been kidnapped and taken to a…place like that." He looked back at Phoebe. "And I was never for leaving the kids with Big Tag. The last time we did Tristan came home and used his bedsheets to rappel down from the first floor to the kitchen because Tag's tiny criminals taught him how."

Tris smiled. "It's more fun than stairs."

Adam shook his head. "Besides, I'm trusting you to run the whole company I've got everything I own invested in. I think I can trust you with my kids."

She stopped. "I'm sorry. What did you say?"

But they were already hurrying out. Jake waved. "He said we trust you two implicitly. We'll call you when we get in."

"If they have phones there," Adam said with a shake of his head. "I've heard it's weird."

They were gone.

Jesse smiled down at Brianna. "Your dads are crazy, little girl."

She was stuck on something Adam had said. That whole thing about being in charge of everything… "What did he mean about trusting me with his office?"

Jesse's smile brightened further. "Didn't I tell you about that? We voted to make you the CFO and head up the actual business end of the company. We took the vote at the meeting today. You should have been there. It's going to be awesome, baby. I think this means you're my boss now. I wonder what's going to happen if I miss a meeting."

She sat there as Jesse got on the phone to let their babysitter know they would be just a tiny bit late.

CFO? In charge of all business matters? She'd thought she would have the same job she had here at McKay-Taggart. Accounting. She was a good accounting manager.

She was a good spy.

She'd never been a freaking CFO.

Tristan looked at her with wide eyes. "Auntie Phoebe, what's a nudist?"

Yeah, that was about how her day had gone…

"Baby, what's wrong?" Jesse asked, turning slightly in the seat of their SUV. "You've been tense all day."

She was beyond tense now. Now her head wasn't trying to remember what she'd forgotten. It was worse. She was trying to process what Adam had said. "I didn't realize he was looking for an office manager. I thought I would do accounting. Like I do at MT."

Jesse's eyes drifted back to the road. The kids had almost immediately fallen asleep, which was good because they were stuck in traffic on 75. "It's going to start out with only eight to ten employees, depending on who we decide to hire. You have a killer automated billing system. I don't know how much there would be for you to do with accounting. I'm sure if we grow the business enough, there will be a place for a dedicated accounting person, but it would be too small-time for you. And it's not office management. It's full-on company management."

She hadn't imagined it when she'd agreed to go with Jesse. The Miles-Dean, Weston and Murdoch Investigative Services firm intended to specialize in missing persons and criminal identification. Adam Miles and Chelsea Weston had been working on the software that would not only move facial recognition software to a new level, but also new procedures and processes that would track persons of interest through everyday media.

Leaving McKay-Taggart felt weird, but she'd been willing to because it made Jesse happy to stay with his partner, Simon. They'd been best friends for years, watching each other's back in the field. She'd known when Simon followed his wife to the new firm that Jesse wouldn't be far behind.

It wasn't that they didn't love their work at MT, but this was a whole new challenge. It didn't hurt that they weren't going too far away. They had leased the floor below MT so they didn't even have to find new childcare. It was perfect. They could stay in the family, but follow their passion for finding the missing.

So much time and money had been put into this company.

She could fuck it all up. There was no way Adam and Chelsea's software didn't work. Jake, Simon, and Jesse had been in the field forever.

She was the wild card here. If it all failed, it would likely be her fault.

Jesse's hand came out, covering hers. "Baby, what scares you about this?"

"I have a degree in accounting, but that was a cover." She'd been a spy working for the CIA. The accounting degree gave her access to companies the Agency was interested in. She'd spent years undercover in Asia, keeping watch over some of the world's worst threats.

She'd never managed an office. Never even thought about it.

She'd spent all her time thinking about gathering the intel she needed. Well, that and staying alive. She'd thought a lot about that, and then she'd thought about dying after she'd lost her first husband.

She'd spent so much time thinking about taking things apart she wasn't sure she could keep something together.

Before she could answer Jesse, her phone rang. She looked at the ID. Jake. "Hey, Jake. What's going on?"

"I need to know if we have a travel agent right now. I've tried everything and can't get a flight out tonight, Phoebe. Look, I didn't want to say this around the kids, but Serena's been going through some things and it seems like it's all coming to a tipping point out in that little town."

She knew Serena's problems well. Phoebe felt for her, and now Serena was stuck in small town Colorado and Jake and Adam couldn't get there. "I'll get back to you in a few minutes. Don't freak out. It's going to be all right."

"Can't get a flight out?" Jesse asked as she hung up and started punching in another number.

"I'll get them where they need to go. Hey, Mia. It's Phoebe. I have to ask a favor of you," she began.

Twenty minutes later she hung up with Jake after setting up an elaborate line of dominoes that ended with Jake and Adam getting into tiny Bliss, Colorado, sometime in the early morning hours.

She glanced up and saw they were turning on to the street where they lived.

How far she'd come from that little lost girl who'd met Ten and Jamie all those years ago. She glanced around the suburban neighborhood they'd moved to before Jamie was born. She'd grown up in dirty tenement buildings because her mother had been addicted to drugs. After she'd died, Phoebe had spent her time in foster care. Even there, even when she'd found a small family, there had been expectations. She had never truly felt at home in Franklin Grant's privileged world.

It wasn't until she came to Dallas and met Jesse Murdoch that she truly found her place in the world.

Was she ready for that to change?

Jesse pulled the car into the driveway, bringing it to a stop. "So tell me why you don't want the job. If we wait until we walk in the door, Tristan and Brianna will wake up, and Tris is going to need supervision because no matter what Adam says about Tag's kids, Tris is a hell-raiser, too. He's already started pulling apart electronics to try to figure out how they work. I'll spend all night trying to save our remote controls. So I'm going to need an answer now, baby. I'm worried about you."

How to make him understand? "I've only ever run an accounting department, Jesse. This is a huge change. It's all a huge change. Adam and Chelsea are basically putting their life's work into my hands, and it scares the crap out of me."

He reached out, his big palm covering the side of her face. "I know exactly what you mean. I've never been anything but cannon fodder…"

"Jesse." She couldn't let him go down that road again.

He shook his head. "Sorry. Force of habit. Before I came to McKay-Taggart, I was nothing but cannon fodder. I was there to take the bullets, and I didn't think I could do anything else with my life. You are way bigger than the box the CIA put you in, Phoebe Murdoch. You can handle this. There was never any question who they wanted running the business end of this company. It was always you. And I am going to stretch myself and use my brain. Turns out it's not half bad when I trust my instincts. We're going to do some good in this world, you and I. You'll be magnificent. You always are."

He leaned over and pressed his lips to hers, heat rising inside her the way it always did when Jesse touched her. He'd changed so much since they'd first met, his confidence soaring as he came into his own.

Perhaps it was time to come into hers.

Or it was time to make out in the car.

"I think I want to be a nudist, too. Like my momma," a sleepy voice said. "I don't like clothes. They're scratchy."

Jesse grinned against her lips.

She was so going to kill Adam.

Phoebe opened the door and glanced around, horror dawning. It was like something had exploded all over her previously perfect living room. There were magazines and books all over the floor and everything was wet. The cushions were knocked out of the couch and her lamp was on the floor.

Tristan grinned like the imp he was. "This is awesome."

"Wow," Jesse managed as he put Brianna's car seat down. "What the hell happened here?"

It was a disaster area.

"Mrs. Murdoch, I'm so sorry," a familiar voice said. Normally Phoebe took James to work with her, but when he was sick she left him with her retired trauma nurse neighbor. Janie Slater had retired at the age of forty-nine because her husband had hit it wealthy in the real-estate game, but she still missed having kiddos around. Now it looked like she would rather be in the middle of a bloody life or death trauma than where she was. "Dumbledore didn't like his bath. He got into a mud puddle in the back and was too dirty to come in the house. I tried to hose him down but he got away and somehow he got into the house."

Janie was standing in the hallway, James on her hip. Phoebe's baby boy was giggling at the chaos as though it was all he could have asked for.

"I can guess how," she said, eyeing her son, who was often the dog's greatest partner in crime.

Mrs. Slater set Jamie down, her face pale enough that Phoebe worried she'd lost her babysitter. "It was terrible. The dog ran through the house and somehow he knocked over the slow cooker and it went everywhere. No one was hurt, but it's all over the kitchen floor. Well, the parts the dog didn't eat."

Ah, her stuffed bell peppers were trash. And later on there would be other repercussions because the dog had a sensitive stomach. She quickly went through the ingredients to ensure there was nothing that would truly hurt the massive puppy.

The aforementioned criminal sat his hairy butt down next to Jamie. Dumbledore was the sweetest rescue anyone could have found, but he didn't like baths. He was a gorgeous Labrador-Great Dane-Saint Bernard mixed breed. Not that she'd known that little piece of information at the time. He came up to Janie's waist and he was barely nine months old.

The shelter had convinced Phoebe he would be a lap dog when she'd gotten him at the tender age of eight weeks old.

He'd been so small then. So incapable of causing true destruction.

Now he was a massive dog who looked up at her with big old sad and guilty doggy eyes. Like she was going to force him right back out into the streets because of his transgressions.

James reached down to Dumbie, his best friend. Tristan ran toward Dumbie at the exact moment the dog realized he was truly wet and it was time to body shake.

Water went everywhere. And not exactly clean water. Tristan and Jamie seemed to think it was some sort of dance party move. The boys laughed hysterically and the dog continued as though he knew he was performing and the crowd loved him.

Some of the water hit Brianna in her car seat and she began to wail.

Pure chaos. Jesse started to try to reach for the dog, but that wasn't going to work. Mrs. Slater attempted to corral the boys, but they were now trying to shake even harder than the dog.

Phoebe stepped up. "Everyone quiet."

The world seemed to stop. Well, everyone except Brianna, who Phoebe picked up and started to rock. She looked around, quickly forming a plan. "Tristan and Jamie, to the bath, both of you." Jamie's bottom lip poked out, but she was having none of it. "You are covered in dog water, young man."

Mrs. Slater's eyes lit up as though she was happy she could do anything at all to help. "Come along, boys. I'll draw you a bath and get you both in PJs."

"If your bath goes better than Dumbie's, you can have mac and cheese and ice cream and watch a thirty-minute show before bed." Sometimes compromise was necessary to keep things running smoothly.

"Boats! I gots boats, Tris," Jamie promised. "Play!"

The boys ran off, happy with the idea of a bath now.

Mrs. Slater turned. "Mrs. Murdoch, I can't tell you how sorry…"

Phoebe held up a hand. "Don't you even finish that sentence. You are the best thing that's happened to us. I cannot tell you how much I appreciate you helping us with Jamie. Neither Jesse nor I have our moms with us anymore, so you are the closest thing to a grandmother he has. I only hope this craziness doesn't scare you off."

A brilliant smile crossed the older woman's face. "Not at all. It was actually quite invigorating. I miss having little ones. Boys, no running on the stairs. And you could wait until you get to the bathroom to take off your clothes, Tristan."

"I'm a nudist!" Tristan was yelling.

Oh, Serena was going to have fun when she came home. Two problems down.

She turned to her husband. "Would you please grab one of the beach towels and try to get whatever water you can off Dumbledore because Jesse, baby, I'm going to need you to take him to the vet. We can't be certain he didn't wolf down some glass or ceramic pieces when he ate our supper."

Jesse groaned.

She was having none of that either. He was her partner and she managed the house, so he had to take it when she bossed him around. He felt free to do it in the bedroom. "When we took that hairy beast on, he became part of our family, and not allowing him to die because he's a dumbass is our highest priority as pet owners."

Brianna was calming down as Phoebe moved with her. Ah, multitasking at its finest.

Jesse sighed. "Is there even a vet open now?"

How little he knew. "There's an emergency clinic on Maple. He's already registered there. I took him after he ate your tube sock. His leash is on the entryway table and I'll call it all in so they know you're coming. For now I'm going to feed this one and then I'm going to clean up the kitchen, make the mac and cheese, get Brianna ready for bed, and call in a pizza for the two of us."

Jesse leaned over and kissed her. "And you think you can't run a business? Baby, you can do anything. I'll be back after spending a godawful amount of money getting x-rays of our dog's never-ending gut."

Phoebe stood in the middle of the chaos with a smile.

Mischief managed.

* * * *

Three hours later, Phoebe sank onto the sofa beside her husband. He had the news on, two plates with fully loaded pizza slices, and he'd poured her a glass of wine and opened a beer for himself.

She was going to be okay. She could handle everything they threw at her.

"I like that smile on your face," Jesse said. "Is it because the dog managed to survive?"

She cuddled up close to him. This was where she needed to be at the end of a day. A crazy, glorious, wacky day. That was what was ahead of them. Family days. "This is the smile of a confident business woman."

He kissed her, his lips moving briefly on hers. "That's my wife."

His wife. Jamie's mom. The head of an up-and-coming business. It would be hard. It would be imperfect. It would sometimes feel impossible.

And she would manage it.

"Oh, we got a card. It looks like it's from Charlotte." Jesse handed her a pretty red envelope.

Oh, shit. She just remembered what she'd forgotten.

"Babe, it's our anniversary."

Jesse's eyes widened. "Oh, shit."

Well, at least they were in it together.

"Maybe I should be in charge of everything except the calendar." She picked up her wine glass. "To us."

Jesse grinned and grabbed his beer. "To us. Always."

Phoebe sat back. It didn't matter that they'd forgotten. The day was here, one that simply marked the formal date of their union, but she knew it was in the everyday motions that they truly honored their love.

Jesse picked up the remote. "You wanna put on Harry Potter and fool around?"

Yes. Yes, she did.

Slow Cooker Pork Tenderloin with Pineapple

1 (2-3 pound) pork tenderloin

1 cup chicken broth

¼ cup soy sauce

¼ cup brown sugar

1 teaspoon ground ginger

1 (8 ounce) can crushed pineapple

Place tenderloin in a slow cooker. Mix together remaining ingredients and pour over tenderloin. Cook on low for 4 hours. Serve over rice.

Slow Cooker Beef and Broccoli

1 CUP BEEF BROTH

½ CUP SOY SAUCE

¼ CUP BROWN SUGAR

1 TABLESPOON SESAME OIL

2 TABLESPOONS MINCED GARLIC

1 (2 POUND) BEEF SIRLOIN STEAK, CUT INTO 1-INCH STRIPS

2 TABLESPOONS CORN STARCH

½ CUP WATER

1 HEAD OF BROCCOLI, CUT INTO FLORETS

In a small bowl, mix together beef broth, soy sauce, brown sugar, sesame oil, and garlic. Place beef in slow cooker and cover with sauce. Cover and cook on high for 4 hours. After 4 hours, whisk together cornstarch and water in small bowl. Pour into slow cooker and stir to combine. Add the broccoli and stir to coat. Cover and cook 30 additional minutes. Serve over white rice.

Chocolate Cake with Chocolate Icing

Chocolate Cake

3 CUPS ALL-PURPOSE FLOUR

2 CUPS SUGAR

1/3 CUP COCOA POWDER

2 TEASPOONS BAKING SODA

2 CUPS WATER

¾ CUP OIL

2 TEASPOONS VANILLA EXTRACT

2 TEASPOONS WHITE VINEGAR

Preheat oven to 350 degrees. In a large bowl, combine the first 4 ingredients. Then, add the remaining ingredients and mix well. The batter will be thin. Pour into a 9 x 13-inch greased pan or two 8-inch cake pans. Bake for 25-30 minutes.

Chocolate Frosting

1/2 CUP (1 STICK) BUTTER OR MARGARINE, SOFTENED

2/3 CUP COCOA POWDER

3 CUPS CONFECTIONER'S SUGAR

1/3 CUP MILK

1 TEASPOON VANILLA EXTRACT

Melt butter. Stir in cocoa. Add powdered sugar, milk and vanilla. Mix well until smooth. Add a small amount of additional milk, if needed.

Strawberry Pretzel Salad

2 CUPS PRETZELS, CRUSHED

3/4 CUP BUTTER, MELTED

1 CUP SUGAR

1 (8 OUNCE) PACKAGE CREAM CHEESE

1 (8 OUNCE) CONTAINER WHIPPED TOPPING

2 (3 OUNCE) BOXES STRAWBERRY JELL-O

1 (16 OUNCE) BAG FROZEN SLICED STRAWBERRIES

Preheat oven to 400 degrees. In a medium bowl, stir together the pretzels, butter and 2 tablespoons sugar. Press into the bottom of a 9 x 13-inch baking dish. Bake for 8-10 minutes, remove from oven and allow to cool. In a large bowl, using a hand mixer, blend together the cream cheese and remaining sugar. Fold in the whipped topping and spread over cooled pretzel crust. Next, dissolve Jell-O in 2 cups boiling water. Stir in frozen strawberries and allow to set for about 10 minutes. Pour over the cream cheese mixture and spread to cover. Refrigerate for at least 4 hours to overnight before serving.

Sparkling Screwdriver

MAKES A 2 LITER PITCHER

4 CUPS ORANGE JUICE

1 CUP VODKA

1 BOTTLE OF CHAMPAGNE

Mix orange juice and vodka together in a large pitcher and chill for 2 hours. Just before serving, pour champagne in pitcher. Serve immediately. If you are making individual drinks, fill glass 3/4 full with orange juice/vodka mixture and top off with champagne.

Charlotte and Jan's Story

ROUGH NIGHT

"Are you sure this is a good idea?" Charlotte Taggart stared at her husband and then back at the man he'd brought in to handle the night's responsibilities.

Michael Malone looked scared. Michael Malone was a former Navy SEAL/CIA team member who had worked many dangerous missions with a sure and steady hand. He'd grown up on a cattle ranch and spent much of his time on oil rigs. This was not a man who typically looked like he was going to faint.

"I don't know, Malone," her husband said in that tone he tended to reserve for the dumbasses in his life. Unfortunately, according to Ian Taggart, there were a lot of dumbasses in his life. "You think this is a good idea?"

Malone's jaw squared. "I think I need to stop betting against Hutch."

Yep, sometimes her husband was right about being surrounded by dumbasses. Although she'd discovered that even the most intelligent of men could be turned into a dumbass when they gathered in large groups and someone—usually Ian—came up with a fun game. His fun games in the past had included using an ATV to jump over the creek at the back of their property, sending exploding glitter dicks to his rivals, and his favorite, pitting his men against each other in the stupidest of contests. She was worried what they'd come up with now. "What did you make Hutch do?"

Ian shrugged one big shoulder. "It was just a little bet. Hutch and another guy were talking some smack about who could eat more tacos. It was taco Tuesday, so I only spent like fifty bucks on a hundred tacos, and I won us this sweet, sweet babysitting gig."

She should have wondered why there had been cheering and groans of defeat coming from the break room a few days before. She'd been told by Phoebe that if she wanted to keep her belief that their crew had any sense whatsoever, she would avoid that room. Charlie had taken her up on that. Now she knew why Hutch had been downing antacids for days. "Who was he up against?"

Malone's eyes went wide. "Boomer."

Shit. She shouldn't have missed that. Boomer was really just a walking gut who was also one of the world's best snipers. She'd seen Boomer eat quantities of food that would have killed most human beings. "How the hell did Hutch beat Boomer?"

Malone sighed. "I didn't know Boomer had already been to an all-you-can-eat breakfast buffet. But I suspect your husband did."

Ian managed to look as innocent as a rat-fink gorgeous bastard could. "The dude asked for pancakes. What was I supposed to do? And don't play that game with me, Malone. I know you and Case spiked Hutch's coffee with bulk fiber, you assholes."

And that explained why poor Hutch had been in the bathroom for days.

"So Ian bet a night of babysitting and Michael bet what? Also, what did Hutch and Boomer stand to get from this besides heart disease?"

Michael put up a hand. "First off, all Big Tag said was I would owe him one. And all I wanted from him if I won was his Sunday Cowboys tickets."

"I figured if I lost, I would give my seat to Malone and you could have Sunday to go and have a spa day or something," Ian said. "It was kind of a win/win for me. I either got to spend time with you tonight or I got to make sure you had a day off on Sunday."

That man. He was sneaky and manipulative and no one should bet against him. She turned back to Malone, pointing his way. "He wins. He always wins, Mike. And everyone knows what owing him one means."

Malone managed to pale as he looked back at the two girls playing quietly in the living room. "I kind of hoped it would be something like embedding myself in a crazy scientist's clutches for months or joining a drug cartel so we could gather intel. You know, something like that. I could do that."

Coward. Her sweet baby girls weren't...no. She couldn't even pretend in her brain. Those girls were trouble with a capital T, but it was only an hour and a half away from bedtime.

And it would be fun to go out for a little while. It would be nice to play. Ian had announced that he was taking her out after they'd finished a lovely dinner of honey soy pot roast that likely would have lasted for days with a normal family, but her husband knew a thing or two about putting food away, too. Eric Vail was having a play party and they were attending. Between work and kids and all their various projects, they hadn't had a lot of time to play lately. It had been weeks since they'd even been to Sanctum.

A big hand cupped her shoulder. "Come on, Charlie baby. It's one night out and he was a Navy SEAL. He can handle a sleeping infant, two tiny girls, and the mutt from hell."

There was a chime from her phone that let her know someone was on the property. A minute later, Ian was ushering in Boomer. Where Kenzie and Kala had mostly ignored Malone, they lit up when Boomer walked in.

The big guy's face brightened and he suddenly had his burly arms filled with tiny girls. "Hey, boss. Mike said since I failed the taco test, I have to come and help him. Are we babysitting? I thought it would be something bad. Are we going to watch Moana? I love that movie. Especially the chicken. The chicken is hilarious. Hey, do you think we could order some chicken, Mike? I'm a little hungry."

Ian shook his head Michael's way. "Touché, Mike. Well played. He'll eat us out of house and home, but I'm not backing down because Macon is at the play party and he's made lemon tarts. And Charlie can buy some more groceries. She does it all the time."

Charlie sighed. Boys. All of them.

Boomer dropped to the ground and let the girls climb all over him like a jungle gym while Ian explained to Malone what would happen if his precious babies didn't survive the night.

Honestly, she was a little more worried about the men surviving…

An hour and a half later and Charlie was definitely seeing the plus side to her husband's plotting. Sometimes his manipulative side produced awesome results. Though she was a little worried about the chair.

"Are you sure this thing is sturdy? I don't want to break Eric's chair."

She sat in Ian's lap in Eric Vail's beautifully decorated kitchen, waiting for the fun to start. Relaxed. How long had it been since she'd felt so relaxed? Since she'd been able to simply hang with her hubby and not worry about anything more than how long dessert was taking.

They were watching Macon Miles as he put the finishing touches on the dozen or so small lemon tarts he'd made especially for Ian. She always found it fascinating to watch the massive ex-soldier use his huge hands to create delicate treats.

"The chair is fine. Perfectly sturdy enough to hold us both. Come on, baby. Relax. Tell me this isn't fun," Ian growled against her cheek.

"You know I can't." Sitting in her husband's lap, one hand on his chest, was kind of the bomb. She was wearing her favorite corset and a tiny little thong that didn't cover anything at all. She liked it though. After her Master tortured her for a while, he would slide that ridiculous thong off and fuck her silly.

She needed that so very badly.

It was like Ian knew what she needed and had found a ridiculously manipulative way to give it to her. And yeah, that did something for her, too. Her Master was a ruthless bastard who would plot and plan and find a way to have her no matter what it took.

Her cell phone buzzed.

She glanced down. It was a text from Malone.

Okay to make the girls some S'mores? We're having a pretend campout in the living room.

So maybe the billionaire oilman's son wasn't so bad at entertaining the kiddos. She texted a smiley face and a thumbs up and looked back at her Master. Here, that's what he was—the dominant manly Master and she the sweetly bratty sub.

It felt so good to be his submissive for a bit.

A single brow arched over Ian's icy blue eyes. They could go super cold when he wanted them to, and like blue flames when he was hot with desire. "You brought your cell phone?"

She wasn't making any apologies for that, though she had hidden it in the left side of her corset. It fit in right under her arm. She and some of the other moms/subs had sewn in a little patch of matching material to hold their phones in. A little like a holster, but for information and communication, not a gun. Ian could carry the guns. She'd had enough of that for a lifetime. Besides, she knew that sometimes information was way more dangerous than bullets. "Normally I wouldn't, Master, but we're not at Sanctum and our babies aren't with their usual sitter. I trust Malone and Boomer, but the girls…not so much. If they can cause chaos, they will, and they'll giggle the whole time."

She slipped the phone back into her corset.

"Well, I tried Serena but apparently she's busy having a mental breakdown and went to nekkidville, which is somewhere in Southern Colorado. At least that's what Jake said when I called earlier. He and Adam are taking a late flight so they can meet her there. I had to think fast so we didn't get stuck with two more kids and no more sex. They managed to get Jesse and Phoebe to take them, but that meant they couldn't take on ours, too."

Charlie gasped a little. She'd looked at the calendar earlier in the week and sent them a nice card. She tried to keep all the important dates on her calendar. "But Ian, it's their anniversary today."

"I think they forgot, and it is so not my place to remind them. Look at it this way, now they have two more little ones to celebrate with," he said with the smooth smile of a predator who knew he'd gotten away with something. "It wasn't like they were going to do anything special. They would probably watch Harry Potter or something. They can totally do that with the kids."

"That was mean, Ian."

"Well, I didn't remember it was their anniversary," he admitted. "If they forget, how am I supposed to remember? Damn, you smell good."

"I'm pretty sure I still smell like pot roast." She should have insisted on a shower, but the minute she'd acquiesced, he'd bundled her into his truck and started for Fort Worth. She'd found out how carefully he'd planned everything because his kit had already been in the cab along with the bag she usually carried with her to Sanctum.

He ran his nose over her neck, breathing her in. "Yeah, you do smell good enough to eat. I'm going to eat you up later on. I'm going to get you tied down and once everyone is watching because my sub is so beautiful, that's when I'll show them how good you are at taking a cock."

She shivered at the thought because he would take his time and do it all right. He would spank her and warm her up and play with all her parts until she couldn't handle it a second longer.

Charlie couldn't wait.

But she would have to because Macon was holding out the one thing in the world Ian would want to devour even faster than her pussy.

Ian had been on a low carb diet for weeks. His blood work had come back and she'd made him eat better to bring down his cholesterol. Healthy diets made her Master crabby. They had agreed he could break his sugar fast and have a little dessert at the play party.

"Here you go, Big Tag." Macon handed the plate to Charlie and tipped his head. "I'm going to find my wife and tie her up for a while. You two have a blast."

"Thanks, Macon," she said, balancing the tray against her thigh. "You're a lifesaver."

Ian was already staring at the small tarts. "You're the best, Pie Maker. I love you."

She wasn't sure if the last words had been said to Macon or the pies themselves. He'd kind of whispered the words, so she rather thought he was talking to those tarts. She picked one up. Two could play at this game. He would take very good care of her later on. She could make him happy now.

The door to the kitchen came open, but that didn't bother Charlie at all. She was completely looking forward to some crazy exhibitionist sex.

She hadn't known she was an exhibitionist until Ian Taggart had shown her. She could still remember him walking into The Velvet Collar. He'd been the target that night, a young, arrogant CIA operative she needed to distract in order to save her sister.

"God, Ian, you still look the same to me all these years later." The words seemed to slip out of her mouth.

His lips curled up. So often he smirked and she found it sexy, but when that man truly smiled he could light up the world. "That's because I put shit in your coffee to make your sight bad."

She rolled her eyes.

His arms tightened and he got serious. "You're still the same glorious woman, Charlie. I walked into that dungeon and my world flipped. I took one look at you and knew I'd do anything to get a collar around your neck.

You took my breath away. You still do. You will until the day I die and that day, I'll still see you standing there in the dungeon waiting for me."

Her eyes clouded. She had been waiting for him. "I didn't realize what I was waiting for until the first time I saw you. I knew. I knew I wouldn't ever want another man. Come here, baby. You didn't get dessert."

She kind of realized they weren't alone, but again, it didn't matter. When she was with Ian, soft and submissive in his lap, it was easy to shut the world out.

It was Javier and the new girl. Juliana, she thought, but she went by Julie or Jules. They were standing in the middle of the kitchen, staring at the stove. It was a nice stove, but then she wasn't a crazed foodie chef so maybe she didn't get the sexy.

To each his own.

Ian's hands came up, brushing against her cheeks. "No dessert because I knew what was coming. And by coming, I mean you. You're going to be coming, my love. Over and over and over again. You're going to come until I can't stand, until my dick stops working. Take the first bite."

They were practically having intercourse over a lemon tart and she was fine with that. She brought the tart in her hand to her lips. "It smells so good."

"Nothing like how you smell, baby. You smell like sex and mine."

Mine? Oh, yeah, she was his. She didn't want to be anything in the world but his. She licked the tart, knowing full well that he was watching her every move. Hell, she could feel his dick swell under her butt. He didn't try to hide it. That was hers, too. He shifted his pelvis as though trying to make himself more comfortable, but she knew he was really rubbing that massive erection against her. In these moments, he was a horny predatory tiger, rubbing himself against her leg to relieve the tension.

Charlie brought the tart to her lips and slowly took a bite, her eyes never leaving her husband's. They were locked together, bodies touching as she savored the light, tart taste of Macon's finest work. He was a master at turning lemons into perfectly prepared bites of heaven. Charlie licked her lips and then turned the treat her Master's way.

"Only you, baby," Big Tag whispered back.

Charlie loved the look in his eyes as she offered him the tart. She loved watching him enjoy it, knowing all the while that wouldn't be the last treat he would enjoy that evening. Soon she would be the one he was enjoying, her legs splayed and her body at his mercy.

Right before she was sure he would take the tart, he pulled her down instead. His mouth took hers, tongue dominating in a bold move that took her breath away. She relaxed against him, giving him the power in that instant and letting him know she was his to do with as he wished.

Which only worked because she loved him, trusted him, knew he would never do a thing to hurt her.

Only this man. She'd only ever submitted to one man, and even then it was pretty much only sexual. As he kissed her senseless, she wondered where she would be if she hadn't met Ian Taggart. It was funny how in her most desperate moment, her salvation had come in the form of a man who should have been her enemy.

"You taste better than any pie, my Charlie," he whispered against her lips. His hands tightened on her and she felt one of those big palms stroke her thigh. "Why don't you straddle me and let's see what happens?"

She knew what would happen. She placed the tray of treats on the table beside them and gingerly shifted, twisting so she straddled her Master's lap. Yes, there it was. His cock was right against her pussy. All she had to do was…

Ian groaned as she rolled her pelvis. "That's right, baby. Now give me some of that sweet, sweet lemony goodness. Ride me and feed me. That's what I want. Let me watch you come."

"And if I can make you come?" It was a fun little game. She would try to see if she could get that big dick of his to go off before she did.

"Then I'll walk around for the rest of the night a bit on the uncomfortable side," he replied, his hands finding her hips. He shifted and she found herself with her clitoris in the perfect position. "But that's not going to happen. I know exactly how to make you moan, Charlie baby."

She felt her phone vibrate. Charlie winced. "It's another text."

He pumped his hips up against hers. "Answer it. If it's anyone except Malone telling us one of the children is missing, I'm texting them a dick pic and asking them to leave us alone. Let's see if you can text while I do this."

His erection slid over the perfect place and Charlie could feel the orgasm starting to build. How could he still do this to her? All he had to do was start touching her, using that deep Dom voice on her, and her whole body was ready to comply to his any and every whim.

Did she have to answer? It probably wasn't anything important. Was anything in the world as important as the way this man made her feel?

"Give me a taste of that tart, baby. Or better yet, pull those pretty nipples out and let me taste them. Let me lick and suck and bite on those sweet nipples."

Her vision was going soft as he hauled her close.

And her phone vibrated again.

"Ian," she started.

"Do what you need to," he replied as he licked her collarbone. "I'll do what I have to."

She was going to kill whoever was texting her. It was probably Malone, trying to figure out where the damn marshmallows were.

She bit back a groan and reached for her phone. It better be so good because she was getting close, and the minute Ian started sucking on her breasts she wouldn't be able to hold…

Do you have a fire extinguisher?

"What?" Charlie shifted, trying to get a better grip on the phone.

And the chair under Ian kind of exploded.

Charlie hit the floor, her knees knocking on the tile. Ian had gone backward but he'd managed to twist his body so he landed on his shoulder instead of knocking the back of his head against the windowsill.

Panic flooded Charlie's veins. She scrambled to find her phone. "Ian?"

"I'm fine," he groaned. "Call him. Damn it. Can't we have one fucking night out without the world coming to an end? Ah, yeah, this is going to hurt."

Had he thrown out his back again? She couldn't stop and find out. Sarah Stevens was here somewhere and she was a nurse. Surely she could help.

Charlie grabbed the phone from the midst of the now fallen lemon tarts. The tray had turned over, but there were still several that had landed on the table. She would have to shove those in her purse if they were about to flee home. With shaking fingers she dialed the number for Michael.

"Hey, Charlotte, I think I got the fire out. Boomer stopped, dropped, and rolled on it. That did the trick. The girls thought it was hilarious, but we've got another problem now," Michael was saying.

"There was a fire?" She practically screamed the question.

"Tell Boomer to sit on it," Ian said from the floor. "Put him on speaker."

She didn't need his sarcasm, but he had the right to listen in. She clicked to go to speaker. "Where was the fire, Michael?"

"Well, you see when I told the girls we could have a campout in the living room, I kind of thought we would build a fort made out of sheets, you know what I'm talking about," Michael continued, his Texas drawl slow and steady. "Damn, Charlotte. I didn't think the girls would take it so literally."

Her girls took everything literally. "The girls tried to start a fire? In my living room?"

"It was minor," Michael promised. "Mostly because they couldn't take apart the furniture to burn. That was their plan. Apparently Ian taught them how to use whatever's around to stay warm in case they find themselves out in the woods at night. I saved the sofa, but they did manage to get that wicker basket of yours to burn. Kala said she had to use it because she couldn't get to the hatchet."

Charlie turned to her husband. "Why would our daughters know how to use a hatchet?"

He was a nice shade of pale and his shoulder seemed weirdly out of place. "You told me to teach them some life skills."

She was going to kill everyone. Charlie turned her focus back to the man on the phone. "So the fire is out now?"

"Mostly, but there's a problem with a crossbow," Malone admitted. "Basically, Kenzie thought she should provide meat for the fire her sister started. Uhm, long story short, she shot Boomer. It's okay. He gets shot a lot. He's used to it, but I need to know if you have some tarp or something because when I pull this arrow out it's going to get bloody. Should we do it in the garage? And where does Ian keep the first aid kit? Damn it, Kala. Don't play with the arrow!"

"Don't you take that arrow out." She didn't even know where the hell the arrow had lodged. It could be holding one of his arteries closed and when they pulled it out—bam, dead Boomer on her floor.

"You tell him I will kill him if this incident scars my baby girl for life," Ian swore from his place on the floor. "Charlie, baby, my shoulder's out of socket. Could you help me out?"

This was all his fault. He thought it was fun to teach the girls where the freaking crossbow was. And his shoulder came out of socket all the time. It was an old wound. He sometimes jerked it from the socket just to freak people out. Charlie grabbed one of the unspoiled tarts and shoved it in his mouth. "Happy now? I told you that chair wouldn't hold us both and it's the babysitter who got shot. Boomer might die on our living room floor." She was back on the phone. "I'm so sorry. We're on our way right now. Seriously, don't take that arrow out."

She glanced around. They weren't alone. Javier and Jules had walked back in from the backyard and Macon and Ally ran in from the living room. This was not the exhibitionism she'd wanted tonight.

Ian popped up, his arm hanging limp at his side. It didn't stop him from grabbing another tart with his good hand. "Macon! Buddy, I'm going to need these to go. Date night's fucked up again. Javi, some help here?"

Javier shook his head and put out an arm, bracing himself. "Has anyone ever told you you're completely insane?"

Big Tag grinned and used Javier's straight arm to shove his shoulder back into socket with an audible crack. "Never heard that one before. Use condoms. Like three of 'em."

"Call 911," Charlie said into the phone.

"I think I can get the arrow out, Charlotte," Malone drawled. "Especially if the girls kind of help me hold him down. Now that I think about it, we could tie him down."

She heard one of the girls squeal in delight. That was so not happening. "911. Right now."

"How about I call Theo? He and Erin are both pretty decent medics," Malone argued. "Have you thought about the CPS visit that will inevitably come after we call the cops?"

Holy shit. She was going to lose her babies. Tears blurred her eyes.

"It doesn't really hurt," Boomer shouted over the line. "I'm totally stable and everything. Hey, could you pick up some Taco Bell on your way? I'm kind of hungry."

"There's some leftovers in the fridge. Where is he hit?" She was well aware she was walking through a play party. She tried to keep her voice down.

"It was just his leg," Malone said. "No real problem. Not even much blood yet. It went through the meaty part of his calf. And if you're talking about that chicken, yeah, he already found that and ate it. He also ate all your breakfast cereal and four ham sandwiches."

"Damn it," Ian cursed behind her. "Where the hell does he put it?"

Malone continued. "And do you know why the dog keeps whining? I tried to let him out, but he wouldn't go."

Boomer had eaten an entire chicken? And a whole lot of cereal, and then he'd moved on to the deli portion of her kitchen? She might have to let that go. She made it back to the master bedroom and grabbed her purse and her clothes. Those would have to go on in the truck because she didn't have time. "Bud's terrified of coyotes. There's probably one in the back somewhere."

"I can take care of it, Momma!" a delicate feminine voice yelled.

"Don't you dare," she growled into the phone. "I swear whichever one of you little demons tries to go outside and murder the local wildlife will find themselves in a corner for the rest of your life. Do I make myself clear?"

"Dang, Charlotte. She's crying. You made her cry." Malone managed to make it sound like the worst thing that had happened all night long.

"Could you order some pizza?" Boomer yelled. "Don't cry, little girl. I'm okay. Just hungry."

Charlie took a deep breath and looked back at Ian, who was following along.

Yep, she'd been right. Totally bad idea.

"Charlie, baby, you have to see the humor in the situation," he said after roughly twenty minutes of chilly silence. "I mean the girls are barely five and they've got two Special Forces dudes on the ropes. There's some humor there."

This time the chill had come entirely from her direction.

She kept her eyes on the road. She was driving because Ian's shoulder had popped back out of place when he'd twisted the wrong way trying to get to the box of leftover lemon tarts.

"Did you or did you not teach our baby girls, who aren't even in kindergarten yet, how to build a fire?" She knew the answer to the question, but she wanted to hear it from his damn lips.

He turned to her. "How are they supposed to go to kindergarten if they don't know how to build a fire? There are basic skills that are required to live, and I won't apologize for that. They also know how to pitch a decent tent."

Always with the sarcasm. Well, he wasn't the one who had to deal with the public. He wasn't the one everyone judged. "Do you know what they said to their preschool teacher the other day? You're not the one who got called in. I am. I'm the one who has to deal with the teachers."

"What did they do?" Ian asked.

She hadn't mentioned it to him because she didn't want to get mad. There was no way to avoid it now. He should know what his influence was doing. "The teacher told them it was time to come in from the playground and Kala said she didn't want to."

He sighed. "Baby, she's stubborn. You know she didn't just get that from me."

He didn't understand the half of it. "She got the other kids together and explained to them that they didn't have to go in because there were fourteen of them and only one of the teacher."

Ian snorted.

"She talked about how they could flank the teacher and take her out. She made plans in the dirt with a stick. She showed the others how they could overrun the teacher's defenses and take back the playground. I'm not joking, Ian. Miss Mayberry was terrified."

Ian winced as he turned in his seat. "Next time I'll go and talk to the teacher."

That would so put that sanctimonious teacher at ease. Shouldn't a preschool teacher be tougher than that? "And that's going to go so well. You think those girls can do no wrong. Do you know what they did to me at the grocery store?"

His eyes seemed to glaze over. "Well, yes, baby. They decided it would be funny if they played hide and seek with Mommy. You yelled about it for three days. I totally know."

But she was going to tell him again. "They decided it would be funny to hide from Mommy and they pulled out the cereal boxes and hid behind them."

"You called 911," he said, proving he definitely knew the story.

"I called 911."

"You thought our babies were dead."

"I thought our babies were dead somewhere." She still hadn't gotten over the panic. They'd taken years off her life with that stunt. "And what did you do about it, Ian Taggart?"

He held up his working hand as though trying to placate her. "In my defense, I knew they weren't dead. They were right in front of me."

"You laughed, Ian. You high-fived them."

He grimaced. "And that was wrong. I'm sorry, baby. I'm new to this whole parenting thing."

"And I'm not?"

"No, you are not. You've been raising kids since you were a kid. I sometimes feel like a dipshit compared to you."

He did? And honestly, it was rather clever. They'd managed to perfectly conceal themselves and stay off the security camera. They were only five but they'd considered the security cams. She turned on to the freeway that would take them home. "You raised a kid, too."

"Nah, I raised a Sean. He wasn't any trouble. He ate like a horse and he couldn't comprehend algebra to save his life, but he was a good kid. Ours are rotten. Like Chelsea was."

But it was said with a grin.

She would give him that because her sister still called him Satan from time to time. Chelsea hadn't been easy. She'd been hard. She'd been stubborn and obnoxious. It had taken everything Charlie had to keep her sister alive.

Because they'd loved each other. They'd loved each other as fiercely as her twins did. Even at this young an age, Kenzie and Kala had each other's backs. They watched out for each other in a way few children did. Bonded. They were fiercely bonded.

"Oh, god. It's my fault." Her hands tightened on the wheel as the truth rolled over her. "They're not like you. They're like me."

"Well, I did manage to support my sibling in a legal fashion," Ian said quietly. "I worked as a bagger and cleaned up at a fast food joint. You managed to become a teenaged assassin and then built one of the world's most notorious information brokerages. And I find you endlessly fascinating, too. I know it makes you crazy that I love it when the twins do crazy shit, but it's all because when they do it, I am reminded of just how much I love their mother. Their mother is a crazy bitch who rocks my world every single time she enters a room. Their mother is the best woman I've ever met and I want my kids—the girls and the boys—to be every bit as smart and savvy and badass as their mama."

Damn. Now she wanted to pull off on the side of the road and mount him at the first possible time. Mount that man and ride him hard because he was hers and she was his. Because they made badass babies who might bring about the apocalypse and burn the world down, but they were going to be such amazing women someday. Women who could fight for what they believed in. Women who pushed the world forward.

Their daughters.

"You know Miss Mayberry never once mentioned that Kala already has amazing math skills," Charlie said. "That teacher just talked about the bad stuff. How many kids know what it means to set up an army in a flanking position? From what I could tell between the teacher's sobs, Kala's battle plans were nearly perfect."

"Damn straight they were. And I'll give you a better one. That crossbow was locked up in the safe. They figured out my damn password."

A thrill of terror went through her. "Holy shit. I thought one of them was watching me. I took out the Ruger to go with Erin and Phoebe to the shooting range the other day and Kenzie kept making up excuses to stay close. They've been planning this. I shouldn't have let them watch *Brave*. They've been obsessed with bows and arrows since then."

"I...I don't think it was *Brave*." His face was tense in that way that let her know she wouldn't like what he said next.

"What did you do?"

"I thought *The Hunger Games* was about food. You know how much they like watching food talk," he spit out. "It came on cable and I might have fallen asleep. It was right after Seth was born and then they totally blackmailed me so they could watch the second one, but I found out what happened in the third and I got dirt on them so we had mutually assured destruction and they haven't seen *Mockingjay*. No way. No how."

Her babies had blackmailed their father.

She'd blackmailed her dad. Oh, sure, he'd been a horrible Russian mobster who she'd eventually maneuvered into a position where she'd had him killed to save her and her sister's lives, but...like mother like daughter.

"Charlie, baby, I know they make you crazy but they are the best things in the whole fucking world. I love my nieces and nephews—both blood and found—but damn, they're sheep compared to our little psychopaths. Seth is my boy. He's going to be dumb and strong, and he's going to need his big sisters to show him who to beat the shit out of. They're going to run the Agency, baby. I know it. I've already seen Fain looking them over. He's not a weird pervert so I'm pretty sure he's sizing them up as potential operatives. I'll be happy if we can just keep them out of the business through college."

They were super smart. A little ruthless for baby girls. And so much her and Ian.

"And they're marrying Americans. Now that Damon has a boy I have to worry about foreigners," Ian pronounced. "I'm instituting an arranged marriage thing in our family. American males only. No Brits and dear god, no Canadians allowed."

She groaned. He was so obnoxious. "Just because you don't like their bacon doesn't mean Canadian men can't make good husbands."

Almost home. She got off the freeway. Was that a glow in the distance? Had Malone lied and the fire was still raging? Was their house in flames?

Had they gotten the kids and Bud out? Had someone pulled the arrow out of Boomer's leg and he'd bled out on her carpet and they would have to deal with his poor, sad, likely still hungry dead body.

"A civilization's bacon says something about them, and you will never convince me otherwise," Ian replied. "The only thing that could be worse is if one of my precious babies marries a vegan. What the fuck is almond milk, Charlie? Nuts don't have breasts. They don't have breasts."

The truck shuddered and went still, rolling along but without any life.

Oh shit. She glanced down at the display.

"We're out of gas. We have to walk." How could she have forgotten about the gas? Ian had mentioned that they would need some on their way back, but he'd been eager to get to the party. Hell, he'd probably wanted to get there to ensure no one else got a lemon tart.

Her cell phone vibrated. She glanced down.

Please Charlotte. Please. I'll do anything. I can't handle it. It's too horrible.

Her heart sank and she passed the phone to Ian.

He paled. "Park the truck."

She shoved the F-150 into park. She was still in her corset. She'd shimmied into yoga pants but she didn't have her sneakers on. There hadn't been time, and who the hell could put on sneakers while wearing a fucking corset? No one. Not even Dita Von freaking Teese could manage it.

They were blocks from home. They lived in the country. She couldn't walk without shoes. She would have to get out of the corset and Ian only had one working arm.

The world was bleak. Her babies…her precious babies.

Ian came around to her door, opening it and holding out his good hand. "Come on, baby. I'm going to Emmitt Smith this motherfucker."

"What?"

"Emmitt Smith. Dallas Cowboys running back. 1992. It's the last game of the season and the Cowboys need to beat the Giants in order to win a first round bye and home field advantage for the playoffs, but their best player, Emmitt Smith, severely separates his shoulder before the end of the first half. He's got two choices—go to the hospital or suck it up and win. I'm going to suck it up and win, like Emmitt. I'm going to do it for our girls. And our son. Not the dog. He smells."

She gasped as Ian leaned over and put his good shoulder in her midsection, lifting her into a fireman's hold. "Ian!"

"I'll get us home. I'll save our babies from dumbasses and themselves. I'll do it for us, Charlie."

"Emmitt Smith was only holding a football," she pointed out.

"His most precious possession." Ian broke into a jog. "You're mine, baby, and I won't ever fail you. I'm leaving the lemon tarts behind. Be safe, little ones."

He ran, sprinting in a way no man with a separated shoulder who didn't play for the Dallas Cowboys in their heyday should run. His feet pounded the concrete, bringing them ever closer to their home and their devil children who might or might not have murdered Boomer this evening.

"I don't smell smoke," he said as he turned down their street.

It was a good thing. They might still have a house. Three more blocks and they would be home.

"Have I ever told you, you have the sexiest ass I've ever seen." It was right there, his well-toned glutes working in time with his muscular legs. "I love you, Ian. If our children weren't currently attempting to kill their babysitters, I would fuck you right here."

He should know. He should never question where her desires lay.

He was her hero.

"And if I didn't think my baby girls were currently attempting to burn down our house and accidently kill their infant brother, I would fuck you right here, too." He never stopped running. "Yeah, Linkmans, I would fuck my gorgeous wife on your perfect lawn that always gets TP'd because you suck! Go get 'em, whoever you are. Get 'em good."

She looked up and sure enough, there was a kid with a bulk pack of toilet paper standing at the edge of the Linkmans' yard. Was that Johnny Kellerman? It didn't matter because Ian was still running.

He ran past a minivan parked on the street. She was almost certain she knew that van. And it was rocking slightly. Whoever was in that van was having a nice night.

"Who are you?" TP boy asked, his voice hushed. "Is that Mr. Tag?"

"I am motherfucking Emmitt Smith!" Ian screamed and picked up the pace.

She held on as her husband heroically took them home.

She knew they were there when she heard Bud's barking. The door came open and Bud nearly ran them over.

"Thank god!" Malone ran out into the yard.

Ian set her on her feet and she took a moment to reorient.

Malone had Seth in his hands, holding him under his little armpits and as far from his body as he could. "I'm pretty sure the toilet is overflowing because the girls were waterboarding their Ken doll. Boomer is alive but really hungry. The dog vomited on the carpet. Five times. It's okay though because four times he totally ate it again. Only the last one stuck. And this one…god, he smells so bad. So bad. What do I do? How do you live like this?"

"Seth? That last frantic text was about Seth?" Charlie stared at him, her hands on her hips. "You were calm when the girls tried to set fire to the house and nearly killed one of your best friends, but you flip out over a baby's poop? He pooped, Malone. It can be taken care of with a box of wipes and a clean diaper."

"I'm used to terrible things happening. I can handle fires and Boomer getting shot. Been there, done that," Malone admitted. "But not that smell. God, not that smell."

Ian fell to the ground and didn't even whine when Bud started licking him.

Charlie took her baby boy and cuddled him close.

"Situation normal, baby," Ian managed to say.

Yep. All fucked up.

Two hours later, Charlie closed the door and the house was blissfully silent.

Date night had gone to hell, but the damage seemed fairly minimal. The house was still standing. Everyone seemed to be alive, though Malone had complained that his sense of smell had been forever damaged.

Boomer had survived. Theo had come over and stitched the big guy up as he'd enjoyed not one but two large pepperoni pizzas. Theo had some medic training and his wife, Erin, had helped out because… Well, she really liked blood.

The night was over and everything was quiet.

What a fucking day.

She locked the door and moved back into the house. What the hell had happened? Her girls. That's what had happened.

So tired and yet she felt the need to check in on her babies.

She made sure the alarm was on and then headed to the room Kenzie and Kala shared.

No one there. Her heart skipped a beat. Why? Why did she do this? She should have taken the money from all the info brokering and lived a happy, designer clothes-filled life where her children never tried to burn down the house or murder people with arrows or…

She stopped in front of her own bedroom door. Ian was in the middle of their bed, his left arm taped up but still holding on to a baby girl. His eyes were closed, his head on the pillow, his arms filled with babies. Kenzie was on one side, Kala the other, and Seth was happily asleep on his father's bare chest, his diapered rump in the air.

Yeah, that was why she did it. This ridiculous, overwhelming feeling of love was why she went home every night, looking for these amazing people who made up her family.

One eye opened, looking her way. "You coming to bed, baby? Sorry I left you with Theo. The girls were tired."

She flicked the light off. "World domination is tiring."

Even in the low light she could see the way he smiled. "Yeah, it is. It's a Taggart world. My baby girls are princesses, but there's only one queen, Charlie."

Her. This was her house and she was the queen. She settled onto the mattress and cuddled close, one of their twins in between them. All of the warmth of her family encompassed her. They were here. Maybe they were whole or maybe there were even more Taggart demons to come.

Bring 'em on.

She was ready.

Charlie Taggart felt her husband's fingers tangle with hers.

"It was a pretty good night," he said.

She bit back a laugh. "Yes, it was, baby. Yes, it was."

Slice of Life
Karina and Derek in
"Stakeout Takeout"

Slow Cooker Spinach
& Artichoke Dip
Cheesy Monkey Bread
Meatball Sliders
Sausage Ravioli Alfredo
Slow Cooker Stuffed Bell Peppers
Slow Cooker Pizza Chicken
Artichoke Salad
Easy Tiramisu

Faith and Ten's story
Unexpected Gifts

Slow Cooker Spinach & Artichoke Dip

1 (9 ounce) package frozen spinach, thawed, squeezed, and drained

1 (14 ounce) can artichoke hearts, chopped

1 (8 ounce) block cream cheese

1/2 cup mayonnaise

1 cup shredded mozzarella cheese

1/4 cup sour cream

1/4 cup grated parmesan cheese

1 teaspoon garlic powder

1 teaspoon salt

1 teaspoon pepper

1/2 cup milk

Place all ingredients in a small slow cooker and cook on low for 2 hours, stirring every 15 minutes. The dip will be ready after the 2 hours is up. If you're in a hurry, microwave the ingredients in a microwave safe bowl for 1 minute. Stir to combine and add to the slow cooker. Continue to mix every 15 minutes to avoid sticking or burning. Serve with tortilla chips.

Cheesy Monkey Bread

1 CAN REFRIGERATED BISCUITS

4 TABLESPOONS BUTTER, MELTED

4 TABLESPOONS GRATED PARMESAN

1 TEASPOON GARLIC POWDER

1 TEASPOON DRIED BASIL

1 TEASPOON DRIED OREGANO

1 CUP MOZZARELLA CHEESE, SHREDDED

1 (14 OUNCE) JAR PIZZA SAUCE

Preheat oven to 350 degrees. Cut biscuits into quarters. Combine butter, parmesan and spices in a small bowl. Evenly coat each biscuit in butter mixture and place in a greased Bundt pan. Top with cheese and bake for 20 minutes. Serve with pizza sauce.

Meatball Sliders

Meatballs (recipe follows)

1 (24 ounce) jar marinara sauce

1 package potato rolls

1 (8 ounce) package thinly sliced provolone cheese

1/2 stick butter, melted

1/4 cup Parmesan cheese

2 teaspoons dried basil

Preheat oven to 350 degrees. Heat meatballs in marinara sauce over low heat for about 20 minutes. Slice potato rolls in half. Place bottom half of each roll in a 9 x 9-inch baking dish. Place a meatball with sauce on each roll and top with provolone cheese. Place top of rolls on meatballs. In a small bowl, mix together the remaining ingredients and brush over the top of the rolls. Cover with foil and bake for 10 minutes, then remove cover and bake for 2-3 minutes, or until golden brown.

Meatballs

2 pounds ground beef

1 cup Parmesan cheese

1 cup Italian style breadcrumbs

1 teaspoon dried oregano

1 egg

1 tablespoon minced garlic

1 teaspoon dried basil

Preheat oven to 400 degrees. Mix together all ingredients and form into 1-inch balls. Place on a large baking pan an inch apart and bake for 20 minutes.

Sausage Ravioli Alfredo

1 POUND SAUSAGE, COOKED AND DRAINED

1 CUP RICOTTA CHEESE

¼ CUP BASIL PESTO

1 PACKAGE WONTON WRAPPERS

1 TEASPOON SALT

1 (15 OUNCE) JAR ALFREDO SAUCE

½ CUP MILK

Mix together sausage, ricotta and pesto in a small bowl. Separate the wonton wrappers into 2 equal stacks. Place ½-1 tablespoon of filling onto 1 wonton wrapper from one stack and repeat with all wrappers in that stack. Using your finger, wet the outer square around the filling, then place a wonton wrapper over the filling and seal all edges with your fingers. Repeat with remaining wonton wrappers. Boil in a medium pot of salted water for 3-5 minutes. Drain in a colander and return to pot over low heat. Add Alfredo sauce and milk, stir to combine, and simmer for 10 minutes.

Slice of Life

Karina and Derek in "Stakeout Takeout"

8 p.m.

Suburban Dallas

Karina Brighton looked out over the small suburban neighborhood, her eyes carefully watching for any movement. She had to be patient, still. The windows on her van were tinted and she'd parked out of the way, but the smart criminal might be able to see a silhouette moving and decide to take the night off. She did not want that to happen.

This was a favor, not a job anymore. Her job was running a community outreach, but she still remembered how to take down a bad guy or two.

But damn it was way more comfy to do it in a minivan than her old two-seater. She did not care that the guys from MT made fun of her. After Ross had been born, she'd needed a new set of wheels and this minivan had been the safest bet. She'd been a little hesitant at first. After all, it wasn't like Derek was giving up his muscle car so their son could be safe. Mom's sacrifice.

Yeah, Mom's sacrifice was pretty sweet when it came to being comfy sitting for hours.

She had an audiobook to listen to. And she had snacks. No stakeout was complete without snacks.

Where had she put the Cheetos?

Karina nearly screamed when the passenger door came open and a dark figure started to slide inside.

"Hey, babe. Thought you could use some dinner."

She dragged air into her lungs as she looked at her husband. "You should be very happy I didn't shoot you, Derek."

Her hubby. Even after years of marriage and a kid between them, she still looked at that man and wondered how she'd managed to catch a Greek god in her trap. DPD Lieutenant Derek Brighton had been the Dom of her dreams, but he'd exceeded all expectations as a husband and a father.

"Why would you shoot the man bringing you delicious food?" He smiled at her as he settled in. "Look. I went to Top. Though it wasn't on the dinner menu, I convinced Sean to make a couple of burritos. Burrito love. You know you want them."

That heavenly smell hit her and so did a few questions. "Where's our son?"

Derek started to unpack the bag he'd brought. "With my mom."

She frowned his way. "Derek, why are you here? I told you I could handle this. If this is some bullshit about how you're worried about me being alone…"

He held up a hand. "This is some bullshit about me wanting to spend time with my wife. Between that weird case with the body modification dudes and prepping for the review that's coming up, I've been the problem and I know that."

Her heart softened immediately and she reached out, brushing her hand over the scruff of his beard. It was always there at this time of night, that sweet scruff. He would get rid of it in the morning and be back to perfection, but she kind of liked him like this. "You are not the problem. You have a job and it requires your attention. I know that, babe. I don't blame you. I'm the one who let an old friend talk me into a stakeout on what could have been our first date night in months."

His lips curled up. "So we have date night here."

"It could get boring."

He shook his head. "Nothing's boring with you."

Oh, she could show him.

9 p.m.

"Why do all the vampires talk like rappers?" Derek asked. "They are vampires, right? Also what's up with calling dudes 'males' and chicks 'females'? It's odd. And how does the guy with the weird name turn into a T-Rex? Wait. They all have weird names. I need to be more specific."

She paused the audiobook that had been playing through the van. She'd found she could be far more focused on the task in front of her if she was listening and not talking, but Derek obviously wasn't as in love with J.R. Ward as she was. "They have Brotherhood names. And they're a separate society from ours. They don't sound like millennial douchebags."

Derek took a drag off the iced tea in his hand. "Sorry, baby. I guess it's taking me back to that case. Damn I was glad to turn that over to the Rangers. They handle the weird woo-woo shit. You know, I'm actually surprised the press didn't get hold of those killings."

No more audiobook for her. The Brothers would have to wait as she had a much needier male in the car with her. It had been silly to think he could enjoy it when he'd come here to spend time with her. "I think the Rangers are good at keeping the press out."

Derek shifted, glancing out over the darkened street. "You can turn it back on. I'll just listen. Promise."

"Or you could tell me why you're really here, babe."

"I told you. I wanted to spend time with you."

"In a minivan. Listening to paranormal romance and waiting to see if maybe, just maybe someone shows up at the Linkman house tonight?"

He fell silent. "You're here. I thought I should be here, too."

Something was stirring in her husband, but he wouldn't tell her until he was ready. She flipped the button that turned on the radio and quickly found something that might keep her husband's interest. There was a game on. Naturally. There was always some kind of sport taking place in DFW.

His eyes lit up. "The Rangers. Awesome."

Not the ones who had taken over his case. The other Rangers. The ones whose games sometimes took so long she wondered if she was in purgatory.

Well, at least she could focus on the street.

9:48 p.m.

"You want some more? Sean packed a whole thermos," Derek pointed out.

"Nope," she replied. "Rule number one of the stakeout is thou shalt not overfill one's bladder. Not unless one is wearing adult diapers."

He frowned her way even as he poured some more tea into his travel mug. "Adult diapers?"

It wasn't so surprising. "I once had to wait almost fourteen hours to catch a bond runner. He was worth ten k, so there was no way I was letting his ass go. What, you never did your time in a car?"

"We took regular shifts," he replied.

"Princess problems, babe. And if you keep drinking that tea, you're going to have more problems."

He shook his head. "Nah, my bladder's like an iron drum. It can handle a lot."

10:02 p.m.

"You're sure it's the only one available?" Derek asked, sliding out of his seat.

"It's one block that way, babe." She pointed toward the convenience store she'd noted on her way in.

Derek sighed. "Aren't we close to Big Tag and Charlotte's?"

They were, but it was an even longer walk. "Three blocks that way. And I heard they were out for the evening."

His head hung. "Damn it."

Well, she'd told him.

11:38 p.m.

"Are you serious?" She stared at Derek like he'd lost his damn mind.

"I'm just saying that buying an RV could change our lives. Think about it, gorgeous. We could be sitting in our own RV staking this place out," he continued. "We would have our own bathroom."

"I told you not to drink the whole iced tea." He'd been a pampered princess of a police officer for years. He seemed to have forgotten how low rent actual detective work could be.

"Well, it wouldn't have mattered if we had an RV," he pointed out. "We could drink all the tea we liked and not have to risk flesh eating bacteria just to relieve our bladders."

He was such a germaphobe. "I've used the bathroom in that convenience store. It wasn't that bad."

He pointed her way. "You've used the women's room. Men's rooms are completely different animals. Men's rooms are disgusting places where drunk assholes revisit their toddler years and try to paint the walls. You have no idea how hard it is to deal with men's rooms."

"Well, we're not spending a hundred grand so you can drive around with your own personal porta-potty," she argued back.

"But that's the whole point. It's not a porta-potty. It's a state-of-the-art bathroom. I found one with a top-of-the-line bidet included. Think about that. Turn that water to a nice icy cold and suddenly anal has a whole new meaning."

She threw back her head and laughed because he was insane. Although sometimes… "Derek, I think you're forgetting the purpose of a stakeout. It's to blend in. The minivan blends. Your six-figure moving monstrosity of a vehicle would not blend. Not in any way."

He sat back. "I don't know. I just thought if you were getting back into this stuff, maybe we could find a way for us all to be involved."

Was that what he was worried about? She turned in her seat. It looked like the stakeout was a bust anyway. It was almost midnight, and all the incidents up to this point had happened before midnight. "Babe, I'm not reopening the store, so to speak. This is a one-time gig for a friend."

"But I think you miss it."

"You think I miss the long hours and dealing with criminals? The fancy clothes? Wait. I didn't wear those because I often had to kick some ass. Sometimes got my ass kicked, too. Don't miss that either."

He leaned over, his hand sliding into place, fingers locking. "I don't ever want you to miss out on something you love, Karina."

GIRLS NIGHT

Relief flooded her system. This she could handle. "I love my work, Derek. I thought it might be fun to revisit my old days, but honestly even in the minivan, stakeouts suck. I'd forgotten how shitty it is to have to sit in one place waiting for some asshat to finally remember he needed to do a crime. We could have been at home eating burritos and watching TV all snuggled up and happy. I kind of hate this guy now."

"I do, too. I hate all of this," he replied with a smile. "I hated it when I was a beat cop and a detective. I'm too old for this shit."

She leaned over. They'd both been trying to prove how they could have a kid and still be themselves, but the truth was they were different and it was totally okay. "I'm too old for this shit, too. I don't want to eat chips and drink stale coffee. I want my totally environmentally craptastic single cup maker, and I want to actually eat at Top in real life adult clothes and everything. And one day, when we can afford it, we're getting an RV with a bidet."

"God, I love you so much." He leaned over and kissed her.

Reminding her that they hadn't had sex in a while. Heat flashed through her and she no longer cared about a favor for a friend. It was ridiculous and honestly, she knew Teddy pretty well and he likely deserved it.

Derek's hands moved to her hair and he sank his fingers in. He dominated her mouth and the world fell away.

"Come here, gorgeous. I need you so fucking bad," he whispered against her lips. "I know we've both been busy, but I couldn't let another night go by without trying to get inside you."

Yes, that sounded like the best idea she'd heard in forever. Unfortunately, she wasn't sure how they were going to work that…

This was a beautiful, pimped-out mom van, and that meant it was fully functional when it came to reconfiguring the seats. She reached down and let the driver's side fold out as low as it would go. She'd stored the third row because she'd had to restock the center with water and sodas. It was completely empty and as nicely spacious as the dude who'd sold it to them had promised.

It was easy to slide herself off the driver's seat, past Ross's car seat, and into the nice flat space where the third row normally went.

"Oh, I take back everything I said about this car. It's sexy as fuck," Derek said, lowering his seat so he could slide into the back, too. "Although I should point out that our RV would have a bed."

"Hush, you overly luxurious bastard, and get back here and fuck me." She toed out of her sneakers and shoved her yoga pants and undies off her hips.

Derek was already working the fly of his slacks, freeing his cock, though he left everything else on. He fell on top of her, spreading her legs wide.

Who said they were old? They were going at it like two teenagers in a ridiculously expensive, technologically advanced minivan. Okay, so with age came some benefits. She would take them.

Derek kissed her again, his tongue invading. This was what she'd needed. For weeks she'd been restless and when this chance had come up, she'd taken it. Somewhere in the back of her brain she'd thought it would be cool to visit the old Karina, the one who was more concerned with kicking ass than cleaning her baby's butt. The Karina who had worn combat boots and listened to Nirvana and was one of the guys. The one who would never have had sex with her husband in the back of a minivan.

Her old self had no idea what comfort meant. It was warm, fuzzy socks and baby snuggles and a minivan with heated and cooled seats and a backseat meant for fucking.

She wrapped her arms around him as his cock slid inside.

"Oh, god, you feel so good, gorgeous. So fucking good." He whispered the words against her mouth. "How can I miss you every single time we're apart? It's been years and I still hate it when you're not in a room with me."

"I love you, Derek Brighton." There was nowhere she would rather be. "Why don't we make another baby?"

He flexed inside her. "But you're on the pill."

"So we practice for a while," she replied. But she wanted more babies out of that man. He made them right.

Her whole body fluttered as he pulled out and thrust back in.

"Practice does make perfect," he said and settled in.

Derek fucked her hard, the van moving in time to their lovemaking. Yeah, they probably weren't inconspicuous now, but she was way past caring.

She needed this. She needed her husband's cock diving deep inside her because he couldn't stand another second they weren't connected.

"I am motherfucking Emmitt Smith!" someone yelled.

Was there a Cowboys game on?

It didn't matter. All that mattered was the fact that her husband managed to hit the perfect spot and she was the one biting back a scream. The orgasm overwhelmed her, sending her wave after wave of pleasure. Derek stiffened above her and she watched his handsome face contort with his release. He pressed in one last time and then rolled off her, falling to his back.

"Was someone screaming about Emmitt Smith?" He laughed. "This is a weird neighborhood. No wonder Big Tag likes it here."

She liked it here, too. Her body pulsed with the aftereffects, but she managed to get to her knees anyway. That masculine voice had sounded weirdly familiar. She glanced through the back window.

Son of a bitch.

"Gotcha, you little bastard," she said, seeing the punk in the yard she'd been watching over. She was fairly certain he hadn't been the one screaming about running backs, but that didn't matter. She was going to have her cake and catch a little fucker, too.

Derek pushed the button that released the back door of the van.

Karina dove for her pants. "Jeez, baby. Hello, half naked."

He shook his head as he buttoned his slacks. "No time, gorgeous. We've got a perp to catch."

Yes, her perp. Damn man. It was so unfair. Woman had to get totally out of her pants, but all the man had to do was slip 'em down. She cursed her pants as she struggled back into them.

"Hey, you, stop! DPD!"

Karina rolled out and caught sight of their perp. He was standing in the middle of the yard, a roll of toilet paper in each hand. "You Johnny Kellerman?"

Johnny Kellerman, her number one suspect. Fourteen years old. Recently fired from his job mowing Teddy Linkman's yard when he found a service that would do it cheaper. Little Johnny had found his revenge by ruthlessly TP-ing the Linkman yard on a weekly basis.

"Drop the toilet paper," Derek said in his best cop voice.

"I think he needs to use the TP, babe. You made the kid pee himself."

The lights inside the house came on and then Karina found herself playing the boy's advocate.

Forty-five minutes later, they started back toward the minivan, Derek's arm around Karina's shoulders. There had been a whole lot of yelling at first, but she'd managed to work something out that everyone was satisfied with.

"You're pretty good at that, you know," he said with a grin.

"The negotiation thing? I do it every day." She looked up at him. His hair was still mussed from earlier and she loved it when he was just a little messy. "It's part of my new job and I enjoy the hell out of it. I don't miss the private eye stuff."

Not when she could do so much good by being the one at-risk kids came to when they needed help. Johnny was going to provide the Linkman household with free pool cleaning for a month, and if it worked out, he would get hired again. With the promise of no more yard art.

It was a good compromise.

It was a damn good life.

Derek pulled the keys he'd pocketed earlier and pushed the button. Instead of the doors unlocking, the back of the van swung open. "So, Mom has Ross until tomorrow. What do you say we go for round two?"

She hopped into their van. The world could wait a few hours more.

Slow Cooker Stuffed Bell Peppers

6 BELL PEPPERS

1 POUND GROUND BEEF

1 POUND GROUND SAUSAGE

1 VIDALIA ONION, CHOPPED

1 TEASPOON GARLIC POWDER

1 (6 OUNCE) CAN TOMATO PASTE

1 CUP PANKO BREADCRUMBS

2 CUPS SHREDDED SHARP CHEDDAR CHEESE

½ CUP BEEF BROTH

Trim tops off bell peppers; remove ribs and seeds. Combine beef, sausage, onion, garlic powder, Worcestershire sauce, tomato paste, breadcrumbs and 1 cup cheddar cheese in a large mixing bowl. Spoon stuffing into each bell pepper until full. Place peppers in slow cooker and add beef broth. Cover and cook on low for 6 hours. Top with remaining 1 cup cheese and cook for an additional 30 minutes.

Slow Cooker Pizza Chicken

4-6 BONELESS, SKINLESS CHICKEN BREASTS

2 (14-OUNCE) JARS PIZZA SAUCE

1 CUP VIDALIA ONION, CHOPPED

1 CUP MUSHROOMS, SLICED

1 CUP BLACK OLIVES, SLICED

1 CUP GREEN BELL PEPPER, CHOPPED

1 3.5 OUNCE PACKAGE SLICED PEPPERONI

2 CUPS MOZZARELLA CHEESE, SHREDDED

SALT AND PEPPER TO TASTE

Season chicken breasts on both sides with salt and pepper, then place in slow cooker. In a large bowl, mix together pizza sauce, onion, mushrooms, olives, bell pepper and pepperoni. Pour mixture over chicken and cook on low for 6 hours. Top chicken with mozzarella cheese and cook for an additional 30 minutes. Serve over pasta.

Artichoke Salad

1 CUP UNCOOKED LONG-GRAIN WILD RICE

1 CAN CHICKEN BROTH

¾ CUP MAYONNAISE

1 TEASPOON CURRY POWDER

1 TEASPOON WORCESTERSHIRE SAUCE

1 (14 OUNCE) CAN BABY ARTICHOKE HEARTS, DRAINED AND CHOPPED

½ CUP SLICED PIMENTO-STUFFED GREEN OLIVES

1 SMALL BATCH GREEN ONIONS, CHOPPED

1 (8 OUNCE) CAN WATER CHESTNUTS, DRAINED AND CHOPPED

Cook rice according to package directions, substituting chicken broth for water. Let cool. In a large bowl, stir together mayonnaise, curry powder, and Worcestershire sauce. Mix rice, along with remaining ingredients, into mayonnaise mixture. Cover and refrigerate for at least 2 hours to overnight.

Easy Tiramisu

1 SMALL CONTAINER WHIPPED CREAM CHEESE

1 TUB WHIPPED CREAM

½ CUP POWDERED SUGAR

1 TABLESPOON VANILLA EXTRACT

12 LADY FINGERS

2 CUPS BREWED COLD COFFEE

1-2 TABLESPOONS COCOA POWDER

In a large bowl, blend together the first 4 ingredients. Next, place 1 lady finger at a time into coffee and turn 3 times. Place 6 lady fingers in the bottom of an 8 x 8-inch square baking dish and top with ½ of the cream cheese filling. Repeat with the remaining lady fingers and filling. Sprinkle the top with cocoa powder. Allow to set for at least 6 hours, but overnight is best.

Faith and Ten's Story

Unexpected Gifts

Faith looked down at the box and her stomach twisted. The note she'd just read made it plain exactly what the contents of the box contained.

Her sister's ashes.

What the fuck was she supposed to do with those?

Her sister, the one who'd played dolls with her when they were young and gave her makeup advice when they were older. The one who'd ruined countless lives and tried to drag Faith down while she'd done it.

Her sister, the murderer.

The door came open and she started, the sound harsh in the previous quiet of the space.

"Hey, we're back," a familiar voice said. "The boys have done their duty. I've got some gorgeous steaks for the two of us and some mashed-up vegetables for my poor baby boy. That's right, son. You have to have some teeth before you can eat a cow. Hey, baby, are you sure we shouldn't at least let him gnaw on a steak? Maybe that would bring his choppers in."

Her husband. Tennessee Smith strode in, carrying a sack of groceries in one hand and the baby carrier in the other. Her ex-CIA god of a man looked perfectly domesticated with a welcoming smile on his face, his eyes lit with anticipation over the dinner she would cook and spending that time as a family. He'd had little of that in his younger days, and then it had been just him and his adoptive family, and half the time one or more of them had been on assignment. These days Ten Smith tried his damnedest to never miss a family supper.

And then he didn't look domesticated. His eyes took in the box on the table and they went cold.

"Tell me that isn't what I think it is."

She stepped in front of it. She wasn't sure why. It wasn't like her sister had needed protection in life. She certainly didn't need it in death. "It's nothing. Why don't you put those steaks in the fridge? I'll start the marinade."

Ten set the baby down and laid the grocery bag on the table. Grant was sleeping, his little baby body covered in a blanket. He looked so much like his father.

"Let me see the letter, Faith."

Why was she hesitating? She should pass the whole thing over to Ten and he would dump the ashes into a garbage can or maybe pass them off to Theo Taggart so he could piss in them. He deserved that after what Hope had done to Theo. Hope had taken Theo's life and his memories and trashed them all.

Why couldn't she stop thinking about Hope as a small child? Why was she thinking about the time her big sister had helped her learn how to ride a bike and then cleaned the scrape on her knee when she'd fallen off. She could see it vividly. She'd cried and Hope had helped her hop in the house and to the first floor bathroom. Hope had poured alcohol over the wound and then she'd leaned over and blown on it to take away the sting.

Like momma did… she'd said, her eyes solemn because they both missed their mother.

Could a sociopath miss someone?

He stepped in and she had to make a choice. She could give him what he wanted or he would likely simply lift her up and move her out of the way. When Ten decided on a path, he rarely veered from it, and she wasn't about to choose her dead, criminal mastermind sister over her loving husband.

His eyes moved over the note and he cursed under his breath before setting it down again. "Damn it. I told Ezra I didn't want this to happen."

It was a good opening because she wasn't exactly sure what had happened. "Why did they send that to me?"

Her voice was even, as though she wasn't quaking on the inside. As though a million insecurities weren't rising up and threatening to take over. It had come out as a mere query. A curiosity, nothing more.

Ten took a deep breath, seeming to settle himself, and when he looked back up at her, his eyes were warm again. He took her shoulders in his hands and stared down at her. "The Agency kept her body for autopsy. It's something they do in all criminal investigations, but they were particularly interested in your sister. In her brain."

She nodded. "Because she was a known sociopath. I've heard some doctors have been studying the brains of criminals with acknowledged mental illnesses. They're trying to determine if there was an injury to the brain or if it was something that went wrong with the formation. Nature versus nurture. It's the ultimate question when it comes to the criminally insane."

That's what her sister had been. Insane. Oh, she'd been brilliant, but there had been a hollow place inside her that Faith wasn't sure a doctor could see with any amount of testing. She wasn't sure that what had been missing in Hope hadn't been a necessary piece of her soul.

Or was it all about DNA? Had Hope been born bad?

She glanced down at her sleeping son. What would his future hold?

"But once they're done with the testing, they're required to deal with the body," Ten continued. "I told Ezra to take care of it, but something must have gone wrong. Technically they're supposed to do what they can to return the body to the next of kin."

That made sense. "Me. I'm her only living relative."

Because their father was gone. He'd been as bad as Hope. Her father had their mother murdered so she wouldn't give up his secrets.

She was an orphan and that was all right because her family hadn't been the Brady Bunch.

"Faith, talk to me."

She shook her head, going on her tiptoes to plant a kiss on his mouth. "There's nothing to talk about. I was surprised, but that's the extent of it. Could you do something with it? I don't want it in my house."

She brushed past him and picked up the groceries.

He turned, his eyes grave. "I think we should talk about it, baby."

"And I think I have two hungry men to feed," she replied. She wasn't going to think about this. Her sister had died long ago and receiving her ashes meant less than nothing. It was merely unexpected, and that had thrown her. She'd accepted her sister's death long before and it wasn't coming back to haunt her now. "Seriously, it's fine, Ten. I had a long day at the clinic and I'm tired. That's all. Let's have some food and maybe you can open that amazing bourbon Ian sent over and then we can watch some TV or something."

Ten stared at her but made no move to stop her. "That sounds good, baby. I'll think about the 'or something.' Let me know if I can help you in the kitchen."

Such a good husband. Ten was always there for her. "I will."

She strode into their pretty kitchen and started dinner, trying to put that box far from her mind.

Faith hummed as she rocked Grant. He'd fallen asleep probably ten minutes before, but she kept rocking. There was something deeply peaceful about this time of night when the house was quiet and her son was cuddled up in her arms. After she got up and put Grant in his crib, she would join Ten in bed and they would read for a while and inevitably, he would turn to her and kiss her long and slow. Before she knew it he would be inside her and she wouldn't be able to hold back. She would sleep like a baby in her husband's arms.

Unless she lay awake all night worried about the question he'd asked her a few nights before.

How long should we wait? I know you need some time, but I want Grant and his siblings to be close in age. He's eight months now. You think another six months or so? I don't know. You're the doc here. What's safe for you?

He'd been so eager and she'd felt like she'd had the breath knocked out of her body. A sibling for Grant. A brother or a sister. A sibling who might love and take care of him, or who might go totally psycho and try to murder his best friend's lover.

That had seriously been her first thought.

What kind of a mother was she?

Had her own mother looked down at her firstborn baby girl with the same tenderness, never once knowing how wrong it would all go?

Would Hope have turned out different if their mom had lived? Had been able to show her all the love their father hadn't? Would her mother have pushed Hope to be better, to understand that love and compassion were just as important as her big, beautiful brain?

The door creaked open quietly and a big masculine body was silhouetted against the light coming from the hall.

Would she ever get used to how beautiful that man was?

"You need any help getting him down?" Ten asked, his Southern accent slow and decadent.

Ten walked in and she realized he'd lost his shirt. He was wearing nothing but a pair of low-slung jeans, his hair still wet from a shower. He smelled clean and masculine as he leaned over and cradled their son. He easily moved the sleeping boy from her arms to the crib, settling him in before leaning down and kissing Grant's forehead. "You sleep well, son."

She loved watching them together. "When do you have to be at work? Did you get a call from Big Tag?"

It would explain the shower. Her husband worked for McKay-Taggart and they didn't necessarily keep proper office hours. Nor did his job always happen in the US.

He turned and held out a hand. "I'm not going to work. At least not any work that will take me out of this house. Come with me, Faith."

She shivered but not because the air was cool. Nope. It had just gotten hot because his voice had turned dark. Dom deep. She found herself standing up without really thinking about it. Her body obeyed that voice.

When she'd first met Ten Smith, she'd thought she was meeting a Dom she could play with for a little while. She'd wanted three months with him. Now she couldn't imagine not having a lifetime with this man. "What are we doing, Ten?"

"I didn't ask you to question me," he replied. "I asked you to come with me. Unless you would rather sit down and talk. Because I thought you would like some play tonight. I know I need it."

She followed her husband through their neatly kept home. They had two. This four-bedroom here in Dallas, and a cabin near her clinic in Sierra Leone. She loved them both, loved that she got to split her time, that Ten came with her. He understood how important her work was to her.

Would he understand her fears about another child? About the one they had?

Ten opened the door to the small playroom they kept in the house. One day they would have to keep it locked, but for now it was open. He turned on the soft lights.

"You know where you are, Faith. You know what I want."

She knew what he always wanted. Faith immediately shed her clothes, easing out of the pajama bottoms and top she was wearing until she was naked in front of her husband. She sank to the floor, finding her position. There was comfort here. She settled herself, sinking back and spreading her knees wide so she could feel cool air on her pussy. Spine straight. Palms on her thighs. Eyes soft and submissive, focused on the floor and waiting for her Master's command.

Yes, he was right. This was what she needed.

Ten's bare feet came into view. Even his feet were sexy. She knew that soon every inch of his skin would be laid bare to her eyes. Every centimeter of flesh would be open to her touch.

"I've got the baby monitor on. There's no need to worry. I want you to relax. We can hear Grant's every move, but I want you to focus on me and me alone for now. Let me keep an ear open for our son."

She could try to do that. "Yes, Master."

In this room he was the Master. They might have started their D/s relationship in an odd way, but she relied on it in times like this. They were perfect partners outside the bedroom, sharing all the responsibilities of life and making all the decisions together, but inside this room, she gave her body up to her Master.

His feet moved away and she heard the closet door open and then close again. Then she heard the sweet sound of a crop hitting her husband's palm. This was his ritual. He warmed her up with the crop and then they played and fucked and loved for hours.

She shivered when she felt the tip inch up her spine.

"I want to talk to you, Faith."

As long as he fucked her while he did it, yes, they would "talk" all night long. "Sure, Master."

"I want to talk to you about Hope."

All the heat fled her body and she lost her form. "There's nothing to talk about."

He dropped to his knees beside her, seeming more husband than Dom. "Baby, there is everything to talk about and I've neglected it. I didn't want to talk about it because I somehow thought that you were over it, but you're not."

"Over what, Ten?" She wasn't ready for this. She wanted to stay in her happy little bubble for a while longer. But was she truly happy knowing she was keeping something important from her husband? "Over getting my sister's ashes back? Why should that affect me? My sister was a psychopath."

"And she was your sister," he said gently. "Please talk to me. You don't have to start. I'll ask you questions and you can answer and we'll have a nice session. Baby, I wouldn't do this if I didn't think it was important. If you don't want to do it this way, let me call Kai and set up a couple of sessions for us."

Sessions? Her closed-mouth, stoic husband was willing to go to therapy sessions with her. "Why? Why would you do that?"

"Because lately I feel distant from you. I can't stand not being close to you. My life means nothing if you aren't here with me. When we got married Big Tag gave me some advice. He said people naturally grow apart and it's essential in a marriage that someone makes sure we grow together instead. I can't let it go on. I can't sit back and pretend there's nothing wrong."

Oh, what had she done to him? She could hear the pain in his voice, and that had never been her goal. Quite the opposite. She'd hidden her fears in the hopes that he wouldn't have to know, but he did. He knew her and he'd seen past her smiles.

"It's hard to talk about." She didn't want to. She wanted to bury it all and maybe it would go away. Years from now perhaps she wouldn't think about her family and ache with despair.

But she had to make a decision and soon.

"We can talk however you like, but we have to talk. Should I call Kai?"

This was their problem. She was sure Kai would have lots of wise things to say, but at the heart this was between her and Ten, and they had a language of their own. She straightened up, finding her position again.

"No. Let's do this our way." It might not end as she desired, but at least it would be out in the open. "Ask me whatever you would like to, Master."

He stood back up, but she could feel his reluctance. His hand found the top of her head, accepting all she was offering him, promising her he would return her submission with his own gift. "I love you, Faith."

That was never the question. "I love you, Tennessee."

"Then we'll begin." His voice had gone hard again, taking on the persona of the Dom. He ran the tip of the crop up her left thigh, allowing her to feel the leather. "How did you feel when you opened the package?"

"Numb." She still felt a bit numb. "Surprised for a second and then numb."

The crop ran up her body, flicking gently at her breasts. Her nipples hardened, peaking as he stimulated them.

"What was the first thing that ran through your head?"

She wasn't going to lie to him or prevaricate. This was a space where they were always, always honest with each other. Not that she lied to him outside this space, but she might try to spare his feelings. This space in their house, this place in their marriage, was about nothing but their feelings and honesty.

"That I should work quickly because you would be home any minute. I thought I should hide it from you."

The crop stopped and she could practically feel his frustration. "Why? Why would you hide that from me?"

The crop started up again. She closed her eyes and let herself feel the crop, the soft tip of the leather. It was a well-used crop, but it still had a sting. It could still make her skin sing with life. Other wives might want to have this discussion while their husbands rubbed their feet, but this was perfect for her. It was a balance between anticipating his next move and continuing to give him the answers he required. It left no room for measuring her words. They simply flowed.

"Because I didn't want you to look at that urn and think about what happened to you. I didn't want her to bring you another moment's worth of pain."

"You thought you should hide it. Lean over. I want you on all fours, darlin'."

She sighed because that meant he was ready to start in on her in earnest. He knew she was ready, could read the signs of her body. Her skin would have flushed with arousal by now, her body warm and wanting. She did as he asked. "I thought about throwing it away. I thought about tossing it in the garbage, but you tend to take it out in the morning so you might have seen it. I thought about putting it out in the garage, but you cleaned it recently. You would notice a box. Your neat freak really puts a girl in a bad place when she's trying to hide something."

A little brat, so he would start this out right.

The crop came down on her backside, biting into her and making her ache in the best possible way. He slapped it across her ass five times before stepping back.

"Was that the only thing you thought about?"

"I thought about how much it would hurt Theo if he knew I had it. I felt guilty."

"Why would you feel guilty?"

"Because it's in my house." Maybe she wasn't as good with the honesty thing as she hoped she would be. The fact that it had come to her, that she was the only one who could receive her sister's body, marked her in a way she didn't like. And it had brought about feelings she didn't want either, feelings she thought she'd gotten over.

Another five quick swats and she was panting.

"I don't believe you."

He knew her far too well. This was why he was determined to put her in a position where she couldn't run away.

"Trust me, Ten. I was not happy to receive that particular gift."

"Would it surprise you that it doesn't bother me?" he replied. He let the crop run up her spine. "I don't care that it's here. I think we should sit down and figure out what to do with it."

"Throw it away."

"I don't think that's a good idea. I was thinking more along the lines of a very quiet internment."

"Why would we do that?"

"Because she was your sister."

No. Not those words. Those words threatened to break her down, to tear the wall she'd placed into tiny bits. "She was a monster."

"And she was your sister."

"Stop saying that," she ground out.

She heard him sigh and then the sound of the crop cracking on her ass. The sound hit her ear before she felt the actual pain. Again and again. Oh, she would feel this in the morning. She would feel it and the ache would remind her of the connection between them. The weird, wonderful connection that this lifestyle offered her.

He stopped and she forced herself to breathe.

"I can't not say it, Faith. I think it's important. I don't think you wanted to get rid of her ashes because you were worried I might have a PTSD incident. You know I'm over that. Well, as much as I can be. I know she's gone and a bunch of ashes isn't going to send me into a tailspin, but I think it could with you."

"Do you think I want to remind everyone where I came from?" The tears in her eyes felt good. She wouldn't have allowed them before, and that was why this was a better plan than going to Kai's. She would have viewed the conversation as an intellectual one when she needed to put her brain on hold and let her feelings flow. But it was still hard. It wasn't how she'd been trained to deal with things. Her father had taught her to bury everything deep, never let 'em see you sweat.

Of course in her father's case, he also tried to never let 'em see you sell out his country's troops for cash or murder the people who might report him.

"Where you came from? You mean your family? Faith, everyone knows she was your sister."

"Yes, but I don't have to keep reminding them."

"Baby, is this why you're reluctant to go back to Sanctum?"

It had been easier maintaining her friendships while she was in Africa. For roughly a year before Grant had been born, Ten had been working in the region and in Southeast Asia while she'd run her clinic. She'd talked to Erin, come home to be with her when she could, but she hadn't been forced to think about what her very presence meant to everyone else.

Her sister had ruined Theo Taggart's life. How could they stand to look at her?

"I think it's easier to play alone, Master."

He moved to the front and eased her back on her heels, taking a knee so he could see her. "Do you think they hate you, Faith?"

Hate was a strong word. "I think I would make them uncomfortable."

"Erin loves you. No one lost more than Erin."

"Theo did."

Ten shrugged. "Yeah, but he doesn't remember most of it so he doesn't count."

"That's a terrible thing to say." But her lips were quirking despite her own shock.

"I could say many, many worse things," he replied. "Erin considers you her best friend. She doesn't hate you. Neither does Theo, nor do any of the Taggart brothers. They consider you part of the family and that means something to them. I think deep inside you know that. You know you're welcome so if that isn't the real problem, we have to figure out what is. Baby, do you think less of me because of where I came from?"

"Don't be ridiculous."

"I came from a woman who dumped me in the trash can after she gave birth to me because her place in the high school hierarchy was more important than a child to her."

Tennessee had a hard start in life. He'd barely made it through his first day, and it had only been a homeless, hungry vet who had saved him. "Ten, it's not the same."

"Isn't it? My mother was a weak person. She was a drug addict. I think sometimes if Franklin Grant hadn't found me, I would have ended up the same. And yet when we found her grave, you went with me to visit it because you knew that I needed that closure from her. You knew somewhere deep down I had to find a way to let go of my anger toward her."

She shook her head. "You can't expect me to forgive her."

He stood and then lifted her to her feet. "I don't. I do need you to forgive yourself. I need that badly. Grant needs it."

The tears started up again. "Ten, please. Spank me again."

He shook his head, looking deep into her eyes. "I'll only do that when it brings you pleasure. I will not punish you for something you didn't do. You did not know what your sister was capable of. She never showed that side to you. The minute you did know, you helped bring her in."

"I should have seen it. I lived with her. I grew up with her. I…" She couldn't say it.

Ten's eyes softened. "You loved her. Baby, she was your sister and you loved her and she's dead and her ashes are sitting in the living room and it's all right for you to cry. It's all right for you to feel. No one I know feels as much as you do and hides it. Give it to me. It's my right to see your pain and share it. I'm worth nothing at all if I can't comfort you. I always thought I was born to try to protect my country, but this is my true purpose. Loving you. Comforting you."

The words broke her. His hands on her body, warming her. He pulled her in close and she was surrounded by him. This was what he did. He wrapped her in his gorgeous, scarred body and shut away the world.

"Your daddy is the one who told you not to cry. He was wrong, Faith. There is strength in letting go. You have to be able to show our son that—the same way you showed me."

Their son. "What if I ruin him?"

The true heart of everything.

Ten leaned back, searching her face. "Baby, what is that supposed to mean?"

"My sister was a monster. What if…"

He kissed the top of her head. "No. What Hope had, it's not something that gets passed on through DNA. You know that, Doc."

"But we don't."

"If that were true there would be families of serial killers. It's a combination of nature and nurture. Your father saw your sister's nature and he did everything he could to nurture it. He helped mold her into a person without a conscience. He was proud of her, proud of what he'd helped her become. I was there and I saw it. You would never allow that to happen to our son. I'm not saying he couldn't do bad things. He'll be human. But he'll be raised by parents who love him and a whole crazy family who'll put him on his ass when he does something wrong. That baby in there is going to be so surrounded by love he won't ever question his place, and that will bring its own problems."

Because every kid had a unique set of problems. No parent got out without pain and frustration. It was the tradeoff. The ultimate love could cause the ultimate pain.

She'd loved her sister and her sister had disappointed her brutally.

"I'm afraid to have another kid. I'm afraid of putting Grant in my position."

He shook his head. "First off, we don't have to have any more kids, baby. I'm fine with Grant, but you need to make that decision because you're happy where we are and you don't need anything else. You can't make that decision because you're afraid. Not when you have so damn much love to give. You know what I want to do? If I had my way, we would adopt from now on. We would find the lost kids of this world and give them a home, and do you know how risky that is? We'll have no idea what those kids have really been through, how damaged they are. We'll be going in blind and praying."

They would go in with the deep belief that there was nothing so broken it couldn't be put back together with enough love and patience. As his adoptive father had shown Ten.

What if Franklin Grant had been too afraid to take in damaged kids? Where would her husband be without that man's compassion? He wouldn't have had Jamie or Phoebe in his life. He wouldn't have become the man he was.

"I hate the fact that I miss her sometimes." The tears came freely now. He'd found the core of her torment. She'd had a sister who'd done terrible things…but she'd still been her sister. She'd lost her father and her mother.

And she'd never felt like she could cry for them.

Not for them. Her sister was at peace finally, and it was a good thing. Hope couldn't hurt anyone again, and neither could their father. She wasn't crying for them. She was crying for herself, for what she'd lost, for what she'd never really had.

Her family had been an illusion, a wispy figment of her imagination, bolstered by her father and sister pretending to be normal around her. They'd known how to work her, to keep her in the dark.

But she didn't have to stay there. She didn't have to be afraid. All of life was a risk and she had the best partner in the world to take that risk with.

Ten held her, picking her up and carrying her out of the playroom. He walked them into the bedroom and curled up on the bed with her, never letting her go while she cried.

He didn't say a word, merely let her know he was there, that he would always be there.

Slowly, she let go of the poison that had stayed in her system for years.

Finally, when she went still, he kissed her forehead. "There is no one in the world I love more than you, my wife. You know back when I was with the Agency, I had a mentor named John Bishop. He was the single coldest man I've ever met. John Bishop taught me how to be ruthless in a way my adoptive father couldn't. He started training Big Tag, too."

"Started?" He so rarely talked about his CIA days that she didn't even think about asking him where he was going with this.

"Yeah, about six months into Tag's training, Bishop disappeared. We were all pretty sure he'd been killed by the cartel he'd been investigating. The Jeep he'd been using blew up and we thought he was lost with it."

"I'm sorry to hear that."

"Don't be. I got word today that he's surfaced. My first thought was that he'd faked his death because he'd made enough money or found someplace that offered him more power," Ten said. "Deep down, I'd always known any man that ruthless could go bad in a heartbeat. It's what happened to Eli Nelson. He didn't start out as an asshole. Life in the Agency twisted him and he didn't have anyone in his life to help twist him the other way. So when I heard about Bishop being alive, I thought they were going to throw him in jail."

"Is he there?"

A smile crossed Ten's face and he rolled on top of her. She could feel his erection, loved the way his chest met hers.

"Hell no. He didn't fake his death for power. He did it for love. John Bishop fell in love with some crazy granola girl in small town Colorado and he gave it all up. I mean everything, baby. Apparently he's gone vegan for this woman. John "the Iceman" Bishop went all soft and gooey for a girl and he's holed up in a town called Bliss. Baby, if that can happen, there's nothing the love of a good woman can't fix. And you are the best woman I know. After all, you fixed me."

She kissed him, unable to stay away from him a second longer. She'd been foolish to hide her pain from him. They were married, building a family, and part of that was sharing it all. The good and the bad. The joy and the pain. It was theirs and it was selfish for her to keep it all to herself.

He kissed her, time seeming to stop and the world fading until it was only them. Until nothing mattered but the way their bodies entwined, his mouth on hers, chest to chest, toes tickling each other. She pushed her husband's jeans down, greedy for the feel of him inside her.

He was always inside her, always in her mind and heart, and now she needed him in her body, their physical connection bolstering the emotional one.

She gasped as he thrust inside her, wrapping her legs around him and shoving her pelvis up so there was not an inch of distance between them.

"I love you, Faith."

He always talked about how she'd saved him, but he'd saved her, too. Without Ten, she would be alone in the world, having pulled away out of pain and insecurity. Ten wouldn't let her. He wouldn't allow them to grow apart. He would always be here, pulling them back together.

He thrust in hard and she went over the edge, her nails sinking into his back as she called out his name.

Ten tensed above her and gave her everything he had.

He fell on top of her, burying his face in the curve of her neck. He breathed her in. "When you're ready, we'll figure out how to bury her. We won't make a big deal out of it. Just you and me."

Because she would be honoring the sister she'd known, not the one who had tried to burn the world down. Because Hope, for all her flaws, had been family.

"We should think about adopting soon," she said. "I was thinking about…"

"Sahr. Yeah, I was, too." He finished her thought with a smile on his face.

Sahr was a bright-faced six-month-old whose mother had died in her clinic. They'd spent months looking for relatives, but no one had stepped up.

It was time for her to. It was time to really build a family with a man who knew how to love.

"I'll get Mitchell on it," she promised. It would be hard, but international adoptions could be done. "And Ten, I liked being pregnant. I'm not counting that out either."

"I'll take all the kiddos I can get with you," he said, kissing her again. "Any way we get 'em."

He started to kiss her, his hands finding her breasts and warming her body up all over again.

There was a healthy cry from the baby monitor.

Ten groaned. "I take back what I said about kids. They're annoying."

But he said it with a smile as he rolled out of bed and reached for his boxers. Before she knew it, he was back with Grant, hopping into bed and cuddling their son as he devoured a bottle.

"I wouldn't take it back, you know," Ten said, leaning against her.

"What?"

"Any of it," he whispered. "I would walk into that room where your sister was waiting for me a million times because that pain led me here. And there is no place I would rather be."

Faith cuddled with her boys and looked forward to the future.

Texas Caviar

2 avocados, chopped

Juice of 1 lemon

½ bottle zesty Italian dressing

¼ cup mayonnaise

2 (15.25 ounce) cans black eyed peas, drained and rinsed

1 (15.25 ounce) can black beans, drained and rinsed

1 (15.25 ounce) can gold and white corn, drained

1 (15.25 ounce) can diced tomatoes, undrained

1 Vidalia onion, diced

1 bunch cilantro, chopped

½ cup pickled jalapenos, diced

Salt to taste

Place avocados in a large bowl and combine with the lemon juice. In a small bowl, combine the Italian dressing and mayonnaise. Add remaining ingredients to the avocado and mix well. Add in the dressing and mix well. Refrigerate for at least 4 hours, but overnight is best.

Taco Ring of Fire

1 POUND GROUND BEEF

1 PACKAGE TACO SEASONING

1 CUP CHEDDAR CHEESE, SHREDDED

1 (8 OUNCE) CONTAINER SOUR CREAM

2 TABLESPOONS SALSA

2 CANS REFRIGERATED CRESCENT ROLLS

1 (16 OUNCE) BAG SHREDDED LETTUCE

2 TOMATOES, DICED

1 (2.25 OUNCE) CAN SLICED BLACK OLIVES

½ CUP PICKLED JALAPEÑOS, SLICED

Preheat oven to 375 degrees. In a nonstick skillet, cook beef until browned and add taco seasoning and 1/2 cup of water. Simmer for 5 minutes. Allow to cool. In a medium bowl, mix together the ground beef, cheese, sour cream and salsa. Unroll both cans of crescent rolls, separate into 16 triangles, and arrange them, on a parchment lined cookie sheet, in a ring with the short side of the triangles overlapping to make a circle. It will resemble a sun. Spoon mixture in the half of the triangle closest to the center. Bring each dough point up and over the filling, tucking the dough underneath the bottom to secure. Bake for 20-25 minutes or until golden brown. Place ring on a platter and fill the center with the remaining ingredients.

Burrito Love

2 POUNDS GROUND BEEF

1 PACKET TACO SEASONING

1 (8 OUNCE) CONTAINER SOUR CREAM

2 CUPS SHREDDED MEXICAN CHEESE BLEND

8-10 BURRITO SIZE FLOUR TORTILLAS

1 (16 OUNCE) CONTAINER MEXICAN WHITE CHEESE DIP

Preheat oven to 350 degrees. In a medium saucepan, brown ground beef and drain. Return the meat to the saucepan and add the seasoning packet and ¼ cup of water. Simmer for 10 minutes, then remove from heat. Allow to cool for 5 minutes, then mix in the sour cream and shredded cheese. Take a burrito shell and fill with about ½ cup of beef mixture. Roll up by folding both sides in, then rolling to close. Place seam side down in a greased 9 x 13-inch baking dish. Repeat with remaining burritos. Heat cheese dip according to package directions and pour over all of the burritos. Bake for 20 minutes and serve.

Southwest Chicken

4–6 BONELESS, SKINLESS CHICKEN BREASTS

1 CAN DRAINED BLACK BEANS

1 (15.25 OUNCE) CAN CORN

1/4 CUP DICED RED BELL PEPPER

1/4 CUP CHOPPED VIDALIA ONION

1 (14.5 OUNCE) CAN DICED TOMATOES (UNDRAINED)

1 TEASPOON CUMIN

1 TABLESPOON CHILI POWDER

1 TEASPOON CAYENNE PEPPER

1 TEASPOON SALT

1 TEASPOON PEPPER

1 CUP SHREDDED COLBY/MONTEREY BLEND CHEESE

Preheat oven to 350 degrees. Place chicken in a 9 x 13-inch greased baking dish. Mix together remaining ingredients, except cheese. Cover chicken with black bean mixture and top with cheese. Bake covered with foil for 30 minutes, then uncovered for 20 minutes.

Slow Cooker Cheeseburger Meatloaf

2 POUNDS GROUND BEEF

1 VIDALIA ONION, CHOPPED

2 EGGS

1 CUP PANKO BREADCRUMBS

1 CUP KETCHUP

¼ CUP MUSTARD

¼ CUP DILL PICKLE RELISH

¼ CUP MILK

2 TABLESPOONS WORCESTERSHIRE SAUCE

1 TABLESPOON MONTREAL STEAK SEASONING

2 CUPS SHARP CHEDDAR CHEESE, SHREDDED

Line slow cooker with foil. In a large bowl, combine ground beef, onion, eggs, breadcrumbs, ½ cup ketchup, mustard, relish, milk, Worcestershire sauce, steak seasoning and 1 cup shredded cheddar cheese. Form mixture into a loaf and place in slow cooker. Cook on high for 3 hours. Remove loaf from slow cooker using foil and drain off excess liquid. Place in a 9 x 13-inch baking dish and top with remaining ketchup and cheese. Bake at 450 degrees for 10 minutes. Allow to rest for 10-15 minutes before serving.

Slice of Life

Tiffany and Sebastian in "After Hours"

Tiffany Lowe stared at the white linen napkin on the floor. Seriously? She brought her head back up and frowned at the man who had dropped it.

Chef Sean Taggart gave her a wicked smile. "I'm sorry, Tiffany. You know it's not really my fault, and this should be the absolute final test of the evening. Well, I believe it's the final one your husband set up with the crew. I suspect he's got something planned for you after I leave."

Yes, they were absolutely going to have a long talk. "Where is my husband? I haven't seen him all night."

"He's in the wine cellar," Chef admitted. "You might not have seen him, but I suspect he's been watching you."

"Watching me take his punishment like a boss." Unfortunately, Sebastian's punishment included shoving a piece of plastic up her ass and making her work an entire shift with it, and then, because that wasn't enough, he had every damn Dom in the place suddenly become butterfingers. They'd been dropping crap all night long, and every single one of them had a reason they couldn't lean over and pick it up themselves.

Javier had dropped his spatula but couldn't even think of picking it up because he was stirring a delicate sauce.

Macon's leg was wonky so he couldn't get that pastry bag he'd dropped, and she should hurry before someone slipped and fell.

Lincoln was having back spasms, and could she please grab the rag he'd dropped so he could wipe down the bar?

Every time she'd been forced to do what she now called the clench and snap. Clench all the way down. Snap back up as fast as she could.

Because her lovely Master/husband wasn't going to beat her at this game.

She pointed at the napkin. "You have a good excuse?"

Chef's eyes glittered with amusement. "I'm the boss. No excuses needed."

Well, at least he was open about it. Clench and snap. Clench and clench and clench and she had it in her hand and she was up.

Plug barely still in place.

She handed Chef the napkin with a smile. She'd done the crime. She was actually okay with doing the time. After all, the crime had been totally funny, and she would probably do it again sometime. "There you go, Chef. Easy as pie."

If Sebastian thought she would be humiliated that all the Top Doms knew she was working a shift with a butt plug in her ass, he was so wrong. She'd told the subs, too. Now she was legendary. She was an anal goddess. Of course, it wasn't all good. Someone had mentioned they should nickname her Anal Retentive after this escapade.

Tiff intended to nip that one in the bud.

Chef placed the napkin on the pile of dirty linens to be cleaned and then took his keys out of his pocket. Top was quiet at this time of night, everyone except the closers having fled for home after a long day's work. "What did you do to piss off the som? The rumor is you questioned his pairing of Riesling with the snapper last week."

She couldn't help but smile. He was her som Dom. Her hot hubby. Sebastian Lowe was Top's sommelier. "Oh, that's part of it, but you know it takes a lot to get Sebastian to really blow. You know that my family came into town, right? Well, after an hour of listening to V talk about how dry toilets will save the world, Berry and I might have slipped out to buy some more wine, but we might have gotten lost at NorthPark, and we might have gone shoe shopping, leaving Sebastian alone with my vegan sister for three hours."

Chef's eyes went wide. "Oh, you should be happy this is all he did to you."

It had totally been worth it. If she had to listen to one more rant about her perfectly fine plumbing, she would have...well, she might have been down a sister.

Chef strode out, waving goodnight, and she locked up behind him.

And they were alone.

The lights suddenly went down. Not all of them, but enough to show her which way the Master wanted her to go. He'd left on a few that lit a path to the stairs that led to the small wine cellar and Sebastian's office.

Music suddenly came over the speakers, a slow, sexy beat.

Tiffany's whole body went warm. That was all it took. She could read that man's moods and thoughts, and he was ready to get down and dirty.

She was ready to get rid of the plug and put something a little warmer up inside.

Tiffany stepped inside the cellar. It was always kept around sixty degrees, so a delicious chill spread across her skin.

Sebastian was leaning against the doorway to his office, his suit coat and tie off. She could see a nice swath of tan skin. "How was your day, my love?"

Her day was getting better and better since he'd lit a couple of candles and there were two glasses of wine poured. She took hers, holding it to her nose so she could savor the rich aroma. Lemongrass and wet concrete.

"Now taste," he said, watching her.

He liked watching her drink wine like some men liked watching strippers peel off their clothes. Pervert. He was her pervert and she knew what he liked. She took a sip.

"Citrus and passion fruit." She took another, longer drink because this was one of her favorites. "This is a Sauvignon Blanc from the Marlborough region of New Zealand."

She was learning to be a wine snob.

"Excellent," he praised.

"See, this would have been perfect with the snapper." And being a wine snob had its drawbacks, including a deep desire to fight for the perfect pairing.

Sebastian's eyes narrowed. "You seriously want to go there after the day you just had?"

She shrugged. "I was good at it. I wore that plug like a champ and kept that sucker in despite the fact that every Dom in the place made me bend over. When you really think about it, I kind of won today."

He threw back his head and laughed, the sound booming through the room. "There's a reason I love the hell out of you, Tiff. Never a dull moment." He moved toward her, his smile brighter than the candles. "So the punishment wasn't so bad, huh?"

She could see the outline of her husband's erection hard against his slacks. What had he been thinking about down here? "That depends. Is the punishment portion of the day over?"

He picked up his glass and took a long drink. She loved it when he did that because it meant he was past thinking about the notes and aromas and clarity. He wanted a drink, wanted to enjoy himself.

It usually meant he was ready to enjoy her.

"Take off your clothes, wife, and we'll discuss it." He watched as she worked the buttons of her shirt. He leaned against the gorgeous oak table where they sometimes hosted wine tastings. The "cellar," as they called this particular room, was dark and moody, intimate. He looked perfect standing in the middle of it all, waiting for his wife to undress for him. "After all, I did spend an entire afternoon talking geo politics with your sister, and she insisted on my trying her organically brewed, environmentally friendly lingonberry wine."

Poor Sebastian. Luckily, she had boobs to show him. His eyes flared as she freed her breasts and went to work on the slacks she was wearing.

"I'm sorry, babe. It was a horrible thing to do and I willingly took my punishment."

"And yet your sisters are still in our apartment."

Which was very likely why he'd volunteered them for after-hours duty. "You know they know we have sex. We can have sex with them in the apartment."

Sebastian shook his head. "Nope. Versace told me she's thinking of going back to college for her master's degree, and one of her avenues of research is human sexuality and its effect on the environment. If she hears us having sex, I'm sure she'll barge in right after and ask us a bunch of invasive questions about our safe sex practices. I'll get a lecture on how our lube is killing the biosphere."

Tiffany's lips curled up as she kicked away her slacks. "Then we'll tell her the worst thing of all."

Sebastian moved in, his hands going to cup her face. "That we're not having safe sex. That we're having crazy, dangerous sex. The kind that ends in babies."

Yeah, it was the best kind as far as she could tell. "I think she would argue it ends in overpopulation."

He shook his head. "It ends up with me having a crazy group of kiddos who look like their mother and make my life hell and totally worth living. Damn, I've missed you."

"It's only been a few days."

He groaned. "Yes. Like I said. I've missed you like crazy."

He lowered his head and his lips took hers in a long kiss. He devoured her, savoring her mouth as much as she'd ever seen him savor a vintage. His hands roamed across her flesh, caressing her everywhere he could touch.

She came alive for him, the way she always did. Only this man could bring her fully to life, and she'd known it when she'd met him. He had taken his time admitting the truth, but luckily for him, she was a patient woman.

And she knew what he wanted, why he'd chosen this particular "punishment."

More like "funishment," since this was going to end in her having one big old orgasm.

She even enjoyed being naked in the cellar because this was Sebastian's space. He was the lord and master here, and that meant she was the submissive. It wouldn't work if she didn't get her way most of the time, but she was totally willing to submit to this gorgeous man sexually because he loved and adored and worshipped her.

When she thought about it that way, it didn't actually seem so very submissive, but she was okay if he was okay.

His hands cupped her breasts and she sighed at the sensation. This was what she'd needed all day. This was why he'd walked into the locker room when he'd known damn well she was alone. He'd walked in and locked the door behind him and then shown her that large butt plug. Even then her body had gone hot, her nipples peaking.

"I miss you every second I'm not with you," she said.

He pinched her nipple, twisting it with wicked intent. "Did you miss me while you were shoe shopping with Burberry?"

Ah, the great shop of '17. "I did. I wish you had been there to tell me how good my legs looked in those Louboutins I didn't buy because they were way too expensive."

They'd been gorgeous and B had bought two pairs. Unfortunately, Tiff had budget constraints.

His hands softened on her skin. "I wish I could buy you everything you want."

She shook her head. "I grew up in that world. It's fun, but it wasn't why my parents loved each other. My dad would trade every present he ever bought her for one more day with her. I had fun playing around in the mall, but I love our lives, Sebastian. I wouldn't trade a single second for a gorgeous shoe. You're prettier than any Louboutin."

He dragged her close. "I love you, wife. You can't imagine how deep you go into my soul."

But she could because that was how deep he went into hers.

His lips descended again and she was lost. Time seemed to still as he dragged her against him and she wrapped her arms around him. This was her guy and her time, and everything was perfect.

His hands moved, cupping her curves and skimming over her. His lips moved from hers down her cheek and neck.

She let her hands wander. His body was her playground. Every muscle belonged to her, every scar was hers to kiss and cuddle and love. He'd lost so much but she gave back to him every single time they made love. She felt him up and good, exploring his body with the robust cheer of a true adventurer. There was always something new to learn about him. She could touch him a million times and still love the feel of his skin under her palm.

She let her hands wander lower, to cup his cock and those heavy balls that were held tight against his body when he was this aroused. She loved the fact that he was still dressed and she was naked, loved how much power she found in something that should make her vulnerable.

Sebastian's head dropped back as she stroked him. "That's right. Don't go easy on me. You know I like you rough."

Rough and soft and everything in between. She stroked him hard, watching his gorgeous face as he got closer and closer to orgasm.

"Stop." His eyes opened and he looked back down at her, his jaw a tight line. "Turn around. Place your hands on the chair. Legs spread. Ass in the air."

A thrill went through her at the sound of his rough voice spouting orders. When Sebastian got all Dommy on her, she knew whatever happened next would blow her mind. Without a single hesitation, she turned and did as he asked.

His big palm found a place between her shoulder blades and he stroked a line down her spine. "So fucking gorgeous and all mine."

All his. It only worked because he was all hers, too. Soon they would have more. More laughter. More love. More everything. She would welcome it all with an open heart.

She felt him move in behind her, his cock lining up. Nope. He wasn't going to take out the plug, the big ole perv. She wiggled her ass, letting him know how ready she was for him.

And he was ready for her. He pressed his cock against her, not bothering to take his clothes off. There would be time for that later because they had this whole place to themselves for hours, and she intended to use them right.

"You're so tight," he groaned as he pressed inside her.

Between him and the plug, she was full. So fucking full. She held on to the chair, letting the sensations flow over her as he began to pound inside her. She clenched down, holding that plug inside, but the motion of his body kept it moving gently, fucking her as surely as his cock was.

Tiffany pressed back against him, taking every inch he had to give her. Over and over she pushed and found that perfect place.

Even as she was going over the edge, she felt him swell inside her, pulling on her hips as he ground himself against her.

He kissed the back of her neck and helped her stand up, turning her so he could drag her into his arms. "You know I'm not done with you. Not nearly."

She turned her face up and let him kiss her, getting her hot all over again.

They weren't done. They were just beginning.

Slow Cooker Chili

2 POUNDS GROUND BEEF

1 ONION, CHOPPED

1 (14.5 OUNCE) CAN DICED TOMATOES, UNDRAINED

1 (15 OUNCE) CAN KIDNEY BEANS

1 (15 OUNCE) CAN TOMATO SAUCE

3 TABLESPOONS CHILI POWDER

2 TEASPOONS CUMIN

1 TEASPOON SALT

1 TEASPOON PEPPER

1 TEASPOON GARLIC POWDER

In a medium skillet over medium heat, cook beef and onions until beef is browned. Drain and add to slow cooker. Add remaining ingredients and cook on low for 6-8 hours.

Stuffed French Toast

3 EGGS

3 TABLESPOONS MILK

1 TEASPOON CINNAMON

12 SLICES FRESH WHITE SANDWICH BREAD

6 TABLESPOONS NUTELLA

6 TABLESPOONS STRAWBERRY JAM

CONFECTIONER'S SUGAR

MAPLE SYRUP

6-8 FRESH STRAWBERRIES, SLICED

Whisk together eggs, milk and cinnamon. Spread 6 slices of bread with 1 tablespoon of Nutella and the remaining 6 slices of bread with 1 tablespoon of strawberry jam. Place the two slices together to make a sandwich. Spray a medium skillet with non-stick spray and place over medium heat on the stove top. Dredge each sandwich in the egg mixture, shake off excess, then place in the pan.

Cook for about 2 minutes on each side or until bread is golden brown. Remove from pan and top with confectioner's sugar, syrup and sliced strawberries.

Apple Turnovers

1 TABLESPOON SUGAR

¼ TEASPOON CINNAMON

1 CAN REFRIGERATED BISCUITS

1 CUP APPLE PIE FILLING

1 EGG

1 TABLESPOON WATER

Heat oven to 375 degrees. Spray cookie sheet with nonstick cooking spray. In a small bowl, combine sugar and cinnamon. Separate biscuits and roll each one to form a 4-5 inch circle. Place 2 tablespoons of pie filling in the center of each biscuit. Brush half of the outer circle with the egg wash (egg and water combined). Fold biscuits over the filling and press with a fork to seal. Prick a hole in top of each one and brush with remaining egg wash. Sprinkle with sugar mixture and bake for 15-20 minutes or until golden brown.

Ice Cream Cake

1 GALLON VANILLA ICE CREAM

1 PACKAGE OREO COOKIES

1 CONTAINER HOT FUDGE TOPPING

1 GALLON OF YOUR FAVORITE ICE CREAM

Allow ice cream to soften. Spread vanilla ice cream into a 9-inch spring form pan until a smooth layer is formed. Next, crumble Oreos by placing them in a resealable bag and rolling them with a rolling pin until you have crumbs. Spread hot fudge topping over the vanilla ice cream, then top with crumbled Oreos. Spread your favorite ice cream evenly over the Oreos and place in the freezer for at least 2 hours or until set.

Blackberry Moscow Mule

MAKES 4 DRINKS

1/2 CUP BLACKBERRIES

JUICE OF 1 LEMON

1/2 CUP VODKA

2 GINGER BEERS

In a blender, mix together the blackberries, lemon juice and vodka. Divide the fruit mixture into 4 copper mugs and top with ginger beer. Each glass should have 1/2 beer each. Enjoy!

Serena's Story

Broke Down in Bliss

Serena Dean-Miles felt the car shake an instant before she saw the lights come on in the rearview mirror.

Shit. Shit. Shit.

She never should have tried this. She'd known before she'd left Dallas that this little writers' retreat was a bad idea. There was too much going on in her life, too much to leave behind. She had two kids now and her husbands were busy starting up their own business. They were a month away from opening and they had a million and one things to do. They did not need her out of touch.

Gripping the steering wheel of her rental that damn straight should be able to handle ninety miles an hour, she started to pull over to the side of the road.

Freaking police. Nope. The police were amazing. She loved all the cops she knew, wrote about them all the time, but some of them were overly concerned with traffic laws. There was no one on the road. No one at all. Who cared if she was a little over the speed limit?

Small town cops with speed traps built to bilk poor, unsuspecting, just-trying-to-get-home-because-everything-sucked-right-now tourists.

She put the rental in park and felt it shudder and go still.

What the hell?

She was not going to cry. She would take her ticket and call the rental company. They had to come and get her. Her flight wasn't until tomorrow anyway. She would still get to her Santa Fe hotel in plenty of time to lay awake in bed thinking about it.

It. Was that what one called a non-thing, a thing that wasn't going to happen again, a lost chance?

Nope. She wasn't going to think about that now because she wasn't the woman who cried when she got a ticket. Of course she wasn't usually the woman who got a ticket.

Deep breath. This was a blip in the road. She would be back to her life and she would move on.

"License and registration, please," a laconic voice said.

She smiled her most brilliant smile and turned to look at the officer. And stopped because she was married, not dead. Even though she was married to two men. She glanced down at his name tag. Sheriff Nathan Wright was one gorgeous hunk of man, but he had a fierce frown on his face. "I'm so sorry, Officer. I'm afraid I'm in a hurry to get to the airport. This is a rental. Should I show you the rental agreement?"

"First you can show me your driver's license, ma'am," the gorgeous cop said. "And there was no reason to turn off your vehicle."

"I didn't actually turn it off. It just kind of died." It was obvious this man was not going to be charmed by her smile. She scrambled for her license, digging through her monstrosity of a purse. "I'm so sorry. I guess I wasn't really looking at the road signs. I was thinking about how time moves differently on different planes, so if someone gets stuck in a painting that leads to a different plane, when you get back, how much time has actually passed? It's a really difficult subject, but trust me, if I don't have a mathematical equation that explains exactly how that goes down, someone will complain and loudly." Where the hell was her license? She had to have it. She'd gotten on a plane and rented a car. She couldn't have done that without a license. What if she couldn't find it? What if she'd left it back in Creede? "They'll do that shouty caps thing that makes me crazy."

"Ma'am, I think I'm going to need for you to exit your vehicle."

She stopped. "Excuse me?"

He'd taken a step back, his mirrored aviators hiding his eyes. "I asked that you exit your vehicle, ma'am. I need to know what kind of drugs you're on."

Drugs? Holy shit. She shook her head. "No. No. No drugs. Not even ibuprofen. I had a couple of glasses of wine, but that was last night. This morning it's been nothing at all but coffee. Some of the other writers might have dosed theirs with Kahlua, but I can't handle that in the morning and I'm trying to lose my baby weight. Not that she's still a newborn. No. I wouldn't leave my newborn to go on a boozy writing weekend. Not me."

"Ma'am, are you going to exit the vehicle?" His hands went to his hips, not quite on the hilt of his pistol, but close enough that her heart rate ticked up.

And it had been racing already. What the hell kind of trouble was she in? Cautiously, she reached over and opened the door, easing out of the vehicle. She held her hands up, trying to show him she was neither on drugs nor packing a weapon. "What would make you think I'm on drugs, Officer?"

"It's sheriff, and all that stuff about time and dimensions makes me wonder. Stand away from the vehicle, please." He started to make a slow turn around the sedan. "You were going thirty miles over the speed limit. You can't produce valid identification and you mentioned different planes, and I don't think you were talking about aircraft, were you, ma'am?"

"No, but I can easily explain that."

The sheriff held up a hand. "No need for explanation. You think I haven't worked enough Woo Woo Festivals that I can't tell your kind?" He peered into the backseat window. "It's not Woo Woo Fest time and the sasquatches don't mate until spring, so I'm going to need to know what you're really here for, ma'am."

She could answer him but she wasn't sure she appreciated what he was doing. Yes, she'd been going a little fast, but she still had rights. "I don't think you can legally search my vehicle, Sheriff. I know my rights."

His head came up, his jaw tightening. If he hadn't obviously been the bad guy of the piece, she would have sworn he was the heroic all-American type. He pulled his aviators off and his gorgeous blue eyes narrowed. "Are you a lawyer?"

Somehow she sensed being a lawyer might be worse than being on drugs. "No. I'm not a lawyer. I'm a writer."

He eased back. "Good, because we already have one of those. Gemma got the only exemption. You know there's a town law."

"A law? About lawyers?"

"Yes. No lawyers here in Bliss. Cause too many problems. We work our problems out like real people. The only reason Gemma can practice in Bliss is Nell protested until we gave her an exemption. That worked out real well for Nell, because when I tried to propose a limit on miming protests, Gemma fought it in court and now Nell and Henry are at it all the damn time."

"They protest mimes?" She was starting to get confused.

"No, they use the art of mime as a way to protest man's inhumanity to man or some shit. It's annoying as hell, if you ask me." He looked back into her car. "You sure you aren't on drugs?"

He was big on the drugs. "I'm sure. What exactly are you looking for? Drugs? Because I don't have any. Like I said, I was at a writers' retreat in Creede. My name is Serena Dean-Miles. I know I have identification somewhere. I'm trying to get to Santa Fe where I'm going to catch a plane to Dallas. That's where I live. I think my car is broken down so if you would just give me a ticket, I promise I'll pay it and call the rental company and I'll be out of here ASAP."

He was staring into the window, one hand over his eyes. "You say you're a writer?"

What was that man looking for? "Yes. I write romance novels."

He opened the back door and reached inside.

"Hey, I seriously don't think you have a right to search my car." It was the principle of the thing.

He pulled out a copy of *Love After Death*, with the new cover to match the movie that had recently come out. He looked down at it, studying it and turning it over in his hand. "Tell it to the judge, Ms. Dean-Miles. Wait. We don't have one of those either. We've agreed as a town to have all legal disputes settled by a tribunal once a quarter, unless you're Max Harper and then it's all about the fight club. You wrote this? This picture looks like you."

He held it up as though studying it to make sure it was a match.

She'd only brought a few copies to trade with some of her writer friends for giveaways. She'd come back with exactly one copy. "Yes, it's me."

"This was that movie all the ladies went crazy about," he said, turning it over in his hand again. "The one where the really smart-ass CIA guy's wife comes back from the dead?"

"Yep, that was it." A cautious optimism flooded her system. If she could get out of this by signing a book for this guy's wife, she would call it a win. "I could sign that for your wife if you like."

"And then you'll head out of town, won't you?"

"Yes, then I'll be totally out of your hair." Some small towns didn't like strangers.

He straightened up and seemed to come to some conclusion. Serena got ready to sign and then run as far as she could. She could call a cab. She would go back to Creede. It couldn't be too far. She wasn't even sure where she was now.

"Turn around and put your hands on the vehicle, ma'am."

She felt her eyes go wide. "What?"

"Turn around and place your hands on the vehicle."

"Why would I do that?"

"Because you're under arrest."

"Why?"

He shrugged. "Not sure, but I'll come up with something. Now turn around because I don't want to have to use a taser on you."

A taser? She turned, placing her hands palms down on the hood. It was completely surreal. What the hell was happening? The sheriff gently pulled her arms behind her back and she found herself in real, not cute and kinky, handcuffs. They snicked into place and she was caught.

"Now, don't worry about a thing, ma'am. I'll have Long-Haired Roger come out and take a look at your car. He's a real fine mechanic. Even better since he lost his hair, or so I'm told. By the time I got here, he was already bald. Don't go confusing him with Roger, though. Roger does have longish hair, but he's what I like to call a crazy. Thinks he's going to separate from the States and form his own country. Being as all he owns is ten acres and a trailer, I don't know how he's planning on negotiating for resources, but he tells me I think too small." He started to lead her back to his big SUV. "When we get to the station house, I'll make sure you have your own cell. I got Max in there for being a general asshole. Don't be scared. He's actually a teddy bear but he's got a mouth on him, and sometimes he plays practical jokes that aren't funny. Helping the Farley brothers fly a homemade drone over Mel's place was not a good idea. Mel is our resident alien enthusiast, and by enthusiast I really mean he's a nut job who thinks the Reticulan Greys are on their way. Do you know what he did when he saw that damn drone?"

"Something bad?" This was a dream. A weird dream. She was still sleeping in her little room in the cabin in Creede, and she would wake up and write all this down. It could be a new small town series. The strangest town in the country.

"Damn straight something bad. Watch your head, ma'am. You are precious cargo." He helped her into the back seat. "He launched an all-out assault and ended up not only murdering the drone that was supposed to be the twins' science fair entry, he hit the damn cell tower again. No service at all for weeks. And that's why Max can sit his butt in jail. No pie for him. What kind do you like? I think Stella's got apple and chocolate cream today. Hell, why not go for both?"

She found herself nodding and praying she wasn't about to be murdered in some weird ritual. "Sure."

He gave her a smile that could have lit up a movie screen and then shut the door, hopping into the front and picking up his radio. He pushed the button to talk. "Cam, this is Nate. There's a broke down sedan on the highway coming in from Creede. Can you have Long-Haired Roger haul that into the shop for me? No hurry. I'm coming in now. Get the second cell ready."

Cell. She was going into a jail cell. She wasn't even sure what she was being arrested for except that maybe sanity had been outlawed along with the lawyers.

As the sheriff started to pull away, she glanced around.

"Where am I?"

He looked at her in the rearview mirror, grinning. "You're in Bliss, Colorado, Ms. Dean-Miles. Don't be surprised when Mel or Cassidy shows up and asks you to take the beet. It's no big deal. Just drink a little beet juice and everyone will be so much happier."

"Beet juice?"

"To prove you're not an alien." He pulled out onto the road. "Aliens can't stand the taste. It's a law here that everyone new to town has to take the beet. Don't blame me for that one. The town council planned that meeting during the middle of the Broncos game and no one contested it. I think it's a conspiracy of the big beet farms, but I'm only the sheriff. Now if you're allergic to beets, you can get a medical exemption from the town doc, but be careful. Doc Burke is quick with the colon exam, if you know what I mean."

He kept chatting on about aliens and pies and something about that time the Russian mob invaded, but Serena stared out the window.

Bliss? She didn't know about that. Nothing in her life had been very blissful in months, and a trip to jail wasn't going to change things.

And she really, really hated beets…

An hour later Serena found herself in the second cell of the Bliss County Jail, which was located in the sheriff's office and was as weird as everything else this day had been. One cell was perfectly normal. Bench and nothing else. That cell currently harbored the apparently often-incarcerated Maxwell Harper, another gorgeous man who was wearing Wranglers and a tight black T-shirt. He hadn't stopped complaining about his current predicament or the fact that he wasn't in the second cell.

The cell she'd been shoved into was a veritable paradise, with a cushioned chair, table, and several books and magazines. There was a small bookcase and she was shocked to find ten of her books sitting there amongst the Lee Child and Steve Berry thrillers, and the oddly large amount of books that described how to stop both alien invasions of the world and one's private parts.

There had been a welcome kit waiting for her when Nate Wright had locked the cell, told her to write down her dining preferences, and then stepped away even though she hadn't been fingerprinted or anything.

If she was fingerprinted, then she would go into some online database, and no one in the world was better at finding people via computers than her husband. Adam would find her and then Jake would kick some ass.

How long would it be before they noticed she was missing?

"Hey, lady. Whatcha in for?" Max Harper asked.

She wasn't sure she should talk to him. After all, he was apparently a crazy man who dealt with drones and led teenaged boys into messing with the mentally ill.

Who thought aliens were coming.

And thought beets could stave off the invasion.

She looked down at the menu the sheriff had left behind. There were two, one featuring lunch that would be catered in from someplace called Stella's, and another dinner menu from Trio Bar and Grill.

Was she still going to be here for dinner? And when did she get her phone call?

"I'm not as bad as Nate probably told you," he was saying. "I'm just a misunderstood hero when you really think about it. Whatever you do, don't pick the special. Hal's been experimenting with sushi. It's been a boon for the people doc, if you know what I mean."

Serena sat back, her hand on her belly. It was a force of habit. She'd spent two of the last four years pregnant, a baby growing inside her, feeling him and then her kick and wiggle and thrive. Someone was always touching her belly when she was pregnant. Adam or Jake or sometimes both would sit or lay beside her, big palms covering their child.

She forced her hand away because she wouldn't feel that again. There were no more babies for her.

"Hey, I didn't mean to scare you." Max Harper's voice had gone low, apologetic. "Please don't cry. I can't stand it when pretty ladies cry. And don't think I mean anything flirty by that. I'm a married man and my brother would kick my ass if I ever disrespected our wife like that. I just... All my life I hated to see women scared or crying, I guess. Whatever happened with Nate, once Gemma gets here it'll all get cleared up and you'll be okay. And if Nate's an asshole, then I'll pound on him myself. It's not like I've got anything better to do. Work's slow right now and Rye can handle the horses, so I'll deal with Nate for you."

Serena reached up. She was crying? Sure enough, her cheeks were wet. "I'm all right."

She wasn't. She wasn't even close to all right and she hadn't been for the whole eighteen months since she'd given birth to her last child. Brianna. Her gorgeous daughter who should be enough.

"It's okay. We don't have to talk, but if you have any questions, I know this jail like the back of my hand." The big cowboy sat down on the bench and sighed. "I spend a bit of time in here. It's way better when Rach is here with me though. Jail cell loving has its advantages, but then my brother gets pissed that he gets left out, and Rach gets pissed because when Rye gets nasty, we tend to fight. So maybe it's not so good."

What the hell was wrong with her? She was sitting in a jail cell. A fucking jail cell. When, for the rest of her life, would she be sitting in a cell talking to some cowboy who had said…

"Your wife? Your wife and your brother's wife?"

"Yes," he replied simply. No further explanation.

She needed more information. "So your wife is named Rachel. And your brother's wife is?"

"Rachel."

Frustration welled, but she wasn't about to give up. She would get it out of him. "You both married women named Rachel?"

Max nodded, as though happy she'd finally gotten it. "We both married a woman named Rachel."

Serena bit back a groan and decided to get to the heart of the matter. "Are you trying to tell me you're involved in a marriage where two men share one woman?"

"That's what I've been telling you the whole time," Max replied. "Now it's not as sexy as it sounds. Not according to my Rach. She doesn't think I hear her, but sometimes she tells her friend Jen that two men means twice the soreness. But I'm real gentle. It's Rye who sometimes doesn't treat her right. But I will say when it comes to that kind of thing, it's Callie I feel for."

Oh, she had to know where that went. "Who's Callie?"

Max leaned forward. "Callie's married to Sheriff Asshole, but she's also married to the man who runs Trio, and let me tell you I've seen Zane Hollister nekkid and I have no idea how that man has any blood at all in his brain. Not that I'm a slouch in that department. I do quite nicely there if I do say so myself. I'm just saying there's a limit to what will fit up there and I think Zane's stretching it."

"Maxwell Harper, do you have any discretion at all?" A lovely woman with blonde hair strode in, a cup of coffee in her hand.

Max shook his head. "Not an ounce. Rye got all that discretion stuff and I got the good looks."

The blonde's eyes rolled as she looked over at Serena. "They're identical twins and please ignore Max." She frowned his way. "You know we're not supposed to scare the tourists."

"She's not a tourist," Max shot back. "She's another one of Nate's victims, and she's way more scared of jail than she is marital ménage. I'm trying to make her feel better by talking about the town's least well-kept secret. We have the most polyandrous marriages in the country. We also hold the record for most murders per capita in the world."

"I thought that South American town passed us," the blonde said.

"We shot back up after what Henry and Logan did to those drug dealers a while back. I swear that Colombian town probably sent them up here just for that purpose," Max continued. "So after the murdering thing, we're known for our nudist colony and our happy threesomes. Should I have started with the murders or the big hairy nekkid dudes running around? I rather thought I was doing a good job, Gemma."

Serena stood up. Maybe she was still dreaming, but it was a good one. There was an awful lot of material here.

The woman named Gemma turned to her. "Ms. Dean-Miles, I have no idea what you did that got Nate so excited, but I need to explain your rights as one of the many woefully jailed in Bliss County. I can sue the shit out of this county for you, but all the last person got out of it was a lifetime membership to Teeny's Fudge of the Month club. You're better off going with what I like to call the Don't Sue Us package. It includes a night's stay at the Movie Motel, dinner and drinks at Trio, and a bottle of Mel's tonic, which you might not want because it's rotgut whiskey."

"It's the damn finest moonshine you've ever had," Max explained. "Don't listen to Big City over there. She's got fancy schmancy tastes in everything but men. Her husbands are pure blue collar. They're mechanics."

"Husbands?" Did everyone have two husbands here?

Gemma shrugged. "You know what they say, when in Bliss…"

Serena picked up the little pencil that had been left for her order. The sadness that had enveloped her seemed to lift as she took stock of where she was and what was actually happening here. This was weird. Weird town. Weird people. Weird was awesome. "How about I don't sue if you get me a notepad and keep right on talking. Mr. Harper, how did you meet your wife? Is she from Bliss? Did she come here looking for two husbands?"

Gemma brought over a yellow legal pad and handed it through the bars. "You're easy to please."

How long had it been since she'd genuinely found herself curious? Like super excited to meet someone new and hear their unique stories curious? Probably since the surgery. But now, far from home, she felt that old excitement. There were stories here. So many stories.

"Start talking." She sat down and began making notes.

Max leaned in, his voice deep and rich as he started his tale. "Now that's a real interesting story and I think you'll find I'm the hero. The answer is no. Rach did not come to town looking for two husbands. I think she was a bit surprised by how all that worked out for her. You see, it all started when this waitress walked in the door of Stella's Diner and decided she was in love with me…"

The stationhouse door opened with a little crash. Serena looked up from the notes she was taking about how Max's twin brother Rye had been easily taken out with a child's toy, and Max and their dog, Quigley, had been forced to save Rachel from her evil ex. A petite brunette strode in, followed by the sheriff, who had a stack of books in his hand.

Familiar-looking books.

"I can't believe you, Nathan Wright," the brunette was saying.

A woman with strawberry blonde hair and a baby on her hip strode in right behind the sheriff. "Really, Callie? You can't believe that Nate illegally arrested someone because he thought you would want to meet her? Because if you can say that then you have not met your husband."

"I'm just saying that my husband barely notices what I read," Callie said. "Much less remembers who wrote the books."

"How can I not notice, baby?" The sheriff looked way less arrogant as he fumbled behind his petite wife. "These books are all over the house. You've always got your nose in one."

Callie put a hand on her hip, facing her husband. "Well, Pierce Craig lost his brother to an evil doctor who used a laser to make him forget that he's a Craig. How am I supposed to even breathe until they find him? Pierce hasn't even figured out he's still alive. He's out there all alone and at the mercy of that nasty old doctor."

Yeah, she hadn't even been subtle about that one. It had been far too good a story to not tell. Not that she'd started that storyline until Theo had been home alive and well and finally remembering his place in the world. Erin had even come to her, sat down over some margaritas, and told Serena to just make her look like a badass and they would be okay.

The women of McKay-Taggart knew the power of a good story, too.

"See, I know it's been bugging you and that's why I kept her safe for you," the sheriff explained. "She was going to drive right through and not even stop to say hello." He snapped his fingers. "Gemma, I figured out what I'm charging her with. Cliffhangers. Leaving her readers hanging and making them cry. There's gotta be a law against that. We can hold her here until she frees that character person Callie's worried about."

Yep, she was getting Miseried. They always joked about it, she and Chris and Bridget. They teased each other over margaritas, but she was going to be held in a cell and forced to write.

The brunette turned, pointing her husband's way. "You are not going to Misery anyone, Nathan. And it doesn't matter because there's zero chance that you have my favorite author in a holding cell."

While the sheriff and his wife started to argue, the woman with the strawberry blonde hair walked up to the cell with a frown on her face. The cherubic baby reached out, grinning and calling for Dada.

"No, Paige, Daddy's in a time-out."

Rachel. This was Rachel, the woman who'd had to go on the run, who'd had to change her name and leave her life behind, who'd found the strength to reach out and take her life back.

Of course if she was stuck here for a while, maybe she could write more than one story.

"Now, Rach, you know how prickly Nate gets when he's hormonal," Max replied.

"There is no such thing as male menstruation, asshole," Nate shouted.

"It's the only thing that explains you," Max shouted back.

The little girl clapped her hands as though fascinated by everything going on around her.

Yeah, Serena felt a little like that girl. "Ian calls it mansies."

Max's face lit up. "Mansies. I like it. Nate's got his mansies."

"Gemma, charge her with a 509," Nate said, his mouth a flat line.

Gemma sighed and turned to her computer, but not before tossing back an explanation. "Unfortunately, Ms. Dean-Miles, that is an actual law. Helping Max Harper or Zane Hollister be more sarcastic than they already are is punishable by a thirty-dollar fine."

"Stop that, Gemma." Callie was staring into the cell.

Serena looked behind her, trying to figure out what had Callie transfixed.

"It's you."

Serena gave her a smile. Somehow sitting and talking to Max, hearing his crazy story, had eased something in her soul. "If the books you're talking about are the Soldiers and Doms series, yes, I write them."

Callie stepped forward, tears in her eyes. "But you also used to write Happiness, Montana, right?"

"That was years ago, but yes." They were her first books, the ones where she wrote out all her fantasies of ménage, before she'd found her two perfect men. Before she'd failed them. She tried to shove the thought aside.

Callie stepped up and put her hands on the bars of the cell, her eyes gleaming with tears. "Those books got me through my mother's cancer. They got me through being left alone for six years. They helped me know what I wanted out of life. Even now when the world gets to be too much and I need a safe place to go, I open up your books. Your characters are like a second family to me. I hope you understand what you mean to me."

Now Serena was the one who was teary. "Thank you. I think I needed to hear that today."

Rachel moved beside Callie. "You're really her?"

Callie nodded solemnly. "She is. You look just like the picture on the backs of your books."

Rachel suddenly frowned. "How could you do that to Rio Craig? And his girlfriend, Angel? And I blame the CIA guy. You know, if Tex Jones hadn't gotten caught with his pants down by that senator, none of it would have happened. None of it." Rachel walked over and handed her baby to the sheriff. "You locked up Max. You get to watch our kid, and do not put my precious baby girl in that cage with him or we're going to have a problem, Nathan Wright. I have to go home and get my books for her to sign." She turned, her green eyes narrowing. "Unless you're really going to keep Rio and Angel apart forever, and then maybe we should have a talk."

Rachel was obviously one of those fans. The kind who just might really kidnap an author and hold her in a remote place until said author rewrote the story to Rachel's satisfaction. "No, ma'am. Rio and Angel are absolutely going to be back together. Eventually."

Rachel stared.

"Very soon."

The woman with the strawberry blonde hair made Serena super happy Erin was laid back when it came to her literature. "Good, then. I'll be back. And I'll call the club. They'll all want to come."

"The club?"

Callie grinned. "The 'I Shot a Son of a Bitch' club. We meet twice a month to share information and work through the problems we have because we shot a son of a bitch. We also have a book club and read your stories. You'll like it. There's pie."

"Callie, baby, I think this child has pooped herself." The sheriff was holding Paige out in front of him.

"That's right, baby girl. You're an outlaw. Crap on the sheriff," Max encouraged.

Callie simply walked past him to Gemma and held out a hand. Gemma pressed a key into it. "Nope. You heard Rachel. You incarcerated half her husbands. You get baby-watching duty, and Zane will be here soon so you'll have our twins, too. I'm busting my favorite author out of jail so she can come and meet the women of Bliss."

The sheriff followed after her, still holding the baby at arm's length, but then he had some serious upper-body strength going. "Now, Callie, I did all of this for you."

Callie winked her husband's way. "I know you did and you'll get your reward later. After I've spent some time with my surprise." Callie stopped in front of the cell, using the key like it was something she'd done a million times. The cell door creaked open. "I was only joking, you know. If you need to go, you're free to. I'm very glad I got to meet you. If you've got some time before you need to be on your way, I would love for you to sign my copies. And I sincerely apologize for my husband's illegal jailing of your person."

She could call someone to take her to the airport. It would be an easy thing to do. She could probably bump her flight up and be back in Dallas by this evening.

Or she could try to shove this veil of sorrow aside and find herself again. She could go and meet with women who apparently shot sons of bitches, and then find this Mel person and learn about the aliens. She could stay at a movie motel and see how other trios worked things out.

She'd been dropped in a weird version of paradise and it just might save her.

"I was promised a package that included a night's stay," she found herself saying. "I think I could look around town a bit. And as long as I have some time, I might as well meet your friends."

Callie's smile became brilliant and she reached for Serena's hand. "Come on. I'd love to show you around."

"I have to call my husbands first," Serena said. "Can I use your landline?"

"Husbands? Like a Bliss girl?" Nate asked, his brows rising.

"I told you she's the real deal, and she's in the lifestyle, too. Like Stef and Jen," Callie said.

Gemma pointed to the phone. "Use Cam's. He's out on a call. A bear scared two of the naturists up a tree and they can't get down. I could have told them the bear can climb, too. Dumbasses need a bear kit, that's what they need."

Serena picked up the phone and dialed the familiar number. When Adam's phone went to voice mail, she tried Jake's. His went to voice mail immediately.

This was what they did now. They worked and missed each other's calls and passed their children around. They said I love you to machines because it was too hard to stop down and answer calls. She'd done this. She'd been the one who didn't want to talk about the problem she was having. She'd pushed them away.

"Hey, Jake. I'm in this town called Bliss. My car broke down and the sheriff arrested me, but it was okay because the cell was super nice. My rental is being fixed by Long-Haired Roger who's actually bald, so I'm staying for a while. I love you and I promise when I come back I'm going to be better than I have been in a while and we'll talk. Tell Adam I love him, too, and kiss the kids for me. I'll try to make my plane tomorrow, but it might be the day after. I'm sorry I've been…distant. Bye, babe."

She hung up as Max was refusing to come out of his jail cell.

"Nope. I gotta do my time or I won't be rehabilitated," he argued.

The sheriff was having none of it. "Get your ass out here and change this baby your sperm made."

"How do you know it was me and not Rye?" Max asked.

"You're fucking identical twins. You share sperm," Nate argued back.

"Language, Nate." Callie shook her head and reached for Serena's hand. "You boys have fun. Now where should we start?"

Serena wasn't sure. She wanted to see everything. She walked out into the sun and started to learn about Bliss.

Hours later she sat in a pretty little tavern called Trio, surrounded by a few of the women who had shown up at the impromptu signing. Many of the people of the town had come out. She'd met Marie Warner, who had explained that she did not read Serena's books, but she supported her fully because she'd heard the heroines often shot sons of bitches, and that was good with her. Laura Niles had been a fan, but more of Serena's husband than herself, and that had been a bit of fun, too. Apparently Adam's new facial recognition software was already famous and it hadn't made it to market yet. Laura had explained that she had been an FBI agent at one point and she admired what Adam was doing with his skill. She'd even asked after Alex and Eve, who she'd known briefly when she worked in the BAU.

Serena had more notes than she knew what to do with. She'd met Holly, who was married to an über-wealthy doctor and an ex-Russian mobster. Ex on the mobster part. Alexei Markov was definitely still Russian, and she wasn't entirely certain he wasn't related to Nick Markovic because the two looked an awful lot alike.

Hope Glen-Bennett was married to a rancher and a vet who'd grown up as brothers when their fathers had fallen for the same woman.

And Beth had married a rancher named Bo and one of the NFL's most scandalous players. Serena didn't follow football, but even she knew Trev McNamara's story. The ex-addict had sat in the back waiting for his wife with a cup of coffee in his hand. At one point he'd come up and introduced himself and thanked Serena for all the joy she'd brought Beth.

Why couldn't she feel the same joy?

"I'm simply saying she wasn't the first writer to write a ménage story," Nell Flanders explained. "I wasn't saying they weren't good. Just there are other writers out there."

Nell Flanders had a cup of tea in front of her. Of all the women who had shown up, the pretty brunette with wide eyes and obviously granola tastes had been the only one who'd held herself back. She'd asked a couple of questions about the publishing world and pointed out that not everyone had Serena's wild success.

Serena was pretty sure Nell was a writer, too.

"There are so many out there," Serena said with a smile. She wasn't about to argue with the woman. She'd been told Nell was pregnant, but she couldn't tell from her slender figure. She'd also been told that Nell was having problems with her husband. That Serena could tell. It was there in the dark circles under the woman's eyes. "You can always find someone who speaks to you."

"I don't need anyone else," Jennifer Talbot said, taking a sip of her martini. "You're the bomb, Serena."

"She is. And I can't believe we got to meet you." Callie had shown her all over town, introducing her to the unique residents.

The bar they were in was owned by her family. Her other husband was a massive slab of masculinity named Zane Hollister. He was one of the loveliest men she'd ever seen, and watching him with Nate, bickering like the found brothers they were, made her miss Jake and Adam.

Were they disappointed, too? Did they wonder if one of them hadn't drawn the short stick?

"Oh, there's Rachel." Callie nodded toward the door. "Jen, come with me for a minute. I've got a surprise for Serena I need some help with."

Another surprise? She wasn't sure she could handle much more. "There's no need. I'm actually pretty tired. I was thinking about going to the motel."

But Callie and Jen had already walked away. Leaving her alone with Nell, who didn't seem to like her very much.

Quiet descended, and not the comfortable kind.

"I hear you are very politically active."

Nell's lips curled up in a faint smile. "I am. Well, not as much as I used to be. I can't be chained to trees right now. I rather miss that and some of the things Henry would do before the police got there. He gets very excited at the thought of being discovered by the authorities. But that's neither here nor there. It's not good for the baby so I can't climb up in trees either. I've found that's a useful protest. Well, it was until Max simply cut the tree down from underneath me." She waved a hand. "It was all right. Rachel and Rye caught me in one of those life net things. Apparently the town bought one just for me."

Because the town was crazy…and they seemed to genuinely love and care about each other. Rather like her husbands' work family. Ian Taggart could be the most sarcastic man alive, but he would do anything for his people.

"How far along are you?" Small talk was needed until the others got back. Then she could go to the motel and try to make some sense of her notes. All day as she'd walked around the town, she'd felt more like herself than she had in months. Now she'd slowed down and her doubts were creeping back in.

Especially since they were talking about babies.

Nell put a hand on her still-flat stomach, her skin going a little pale. "Not far along at all. A little over three months."

"Your first?"

Nell was silent for a moment. "I don't know how to answer that. Sort of. It would be my first child if he or she comes to term. I've had two miscarriages, so I don't know if this one will take either."

Serena felt tears pierce her eyes at the hollow tone in Nell's voice. Was she really the one who should talk to her about this? Nell had been pretty negative the whole time she'd been around her. If Charlotte or Grace had been here, one of them would have taken over. She was better at sitting back and observing.

Nell shook her head as though trying to clear it. "You can't write about Bliss."

Serena sat up a little straighter. "You have to admit it's an interesting town. I'm not trying to be hostile or anything, but I can write about whatever I like. I'm sorry if that bothers you. I don't mean to make fun of anyone, if that's what you're worried about. I would honor all the love stories here. I think they're important."

"No, you don't understand," Nell said, biting her bottom lip. "I'm sorry I've been rude. I'm jealous. I hate admitting that. Can I please tell you something that I would prefer you keep a secret? There's a reason you can't write the Bliss stories."

"Because you already wrote them?" Serena thought she had that writer look about her. She'd read a lot of ménage. Listening to Max's story today had seemed familiar, but he'd made himself the hero of the story to the exclusion of all others. Oh, crap. She *had* read it. "You're Libby Finn."

Libby Finn had started out writing pure ménage set in a fictional Western town. She was still with her small press publisher, but lately had shifted toward more romantic suspense. But those first few books…

"I'm sorry I was bitchy," Nell was saying. "It was hard to listen to my friends talk about how awesome someone else's work is. Especially since when they read mine they were very critical. Not that they knew it was mine. It's a secret I hope you'll keep. Rachel thought Rene from *Her Two Cowboys* was too hard on Mac and too easy on Ty. She was very upset that Rene hadn't stayed behind in Dallas and taken out her stalker. She asked me why the character would give up her whole life to go on the run. Which is exactly what she did in real life. I can't win."

Serena knew that well. "Some people aren't very self-aware. And it's far easier to like a book that doesn't hit so close to home. But oh, how I loved your books. I don't know what brought me here, but I know it wasn't just an alternator. You were the first romance I picked up that showed me what I wanted in a relationship."

"I wasn't looking for praise," Nell began, blushing.

"But you'll get it from me." Sometimes gratitude felt even better than praise. Sometimes thanking the people who helped you opened something up inside that was knotted and coiled. "I was in a bad marriage, and your books not only helped me escape when I needed to, they reminded me that I liked telling stories, too. I would think about your characters and would find some of my own. It was like you reached out through the pages and offered me a hand up, so thank you, Nell Flanders. You might not have some major movie deal, but you have people who need to hear your stories. I should know because I was one of them."

Nell reached for a napkin, wiping her eyes. "Thank you. I think I needed to hear that today. And despite my earlier behavior, I love your books. Even my husband has read a few of them. He said Pierce Craig reminded him of someone he worked with a long time ago. Tex Jones, too. I haven't written in a while. I'm too preoccupied with the baby."

Serena reached over and put a hand on Nell's. "I'm so sorry to hear that. I had trouble getting pregnant when I was married to my first husband. Now, of course, I think it was a blessing because he was a horrible man, but at the time I felt useless and empty."

She wasn't about to spout platitudes like *don't worry, this one will be fine* because she couldn't know that. Nell couldn't know that, and there was no way she wouldn't worry.

Nell's hand flipped over and Serena found herself holding it, threading their fingers together like they were old friends—or simply strangers who found a tendril of a bond and wanted to hold on. "But you have children now, right? It all worked out and you're happy?"

Serena went silent. Happy? Had she been truly happy since that moment she'd realized what was going to happen? It had been a blur. One minute everything had seemed fine and the next there had been shouting and Jake and Adam's panicked faces looking down at her before they wheeled her away.

Had she been happy when she'd seen her tiny baby girl, or had she wondered if this baby would cost her everything she had?

So much pressure on a tiny infant.

"I have two, a boy and a girl. I thought I would have more. I thought there would be plenty of time, you know." She shouldn't be talking about this. This was something she kept buried deep and never vocalized because if she did, if she said what she was afraid of, then it could be real.

"You're still young." Nell's hand tightened around hers as though she knew how much Serena needed the support.

"But I can't have more babies. Something went wrong with my daughter's birth and I can't… They took my uterus. I only have one ovary left. I can adopt, but…" The words were shaky. Somehow when she'd talked to Kai—the resident therapist—she'd been able to smile and say all the right things. She'd been able to tell him that she was satisfied with the family she had and she didn't need more. She hadn't cried and Kai had praised her for her rationality.

And told her that when she was ready, when the pain couldn't be held off a second longer, that she should let it go. Anytime, anywhere, he'd said. If she needed him, he would be there.

What she'd been able to keep from Kai, from her husbands, she couldn't hold back now. She'd breezed through it right after Brianna had been born. She'd said if they wanted one more kiddo, they could adopt. And they could. Adoption didn't solve her problem. Adoption couldn't make things right and fair.

The dam was breaking and she was going to look like such a fool. Walking around town, seeing all the happy trios with their kids had softened her up, had made her long for more.

"Nell, what did you do?" Rachel was standing with Jen and Callie, all three women looking concerned.

"Serena, are you all right?" Callie asked. She put down what she'd been holding. "It's a lemon icebox pie. Pierce Craig's favorite. I thought you would like it, so I had Stella make one special, but she's got chocolate, too."

"This isn't about pie, Callie." Jen slid in beside her while Rachel and Callie took places across the table. Jen put a hand on Serena's free one. "I remember when I broke down. It was four days after I got here and I'd just moved into the tiny apartment above the diner. I'd come off a shift and Stella had taken me aside to make sure I had everything I needed upstairs.

She'd noticed I didn't have many clothes or possessions at all really. Just what was in my backpack. The town had gotten together and gave me a three hundred dollar gift certificate so I could buy some new shoes and jeans and stuff. I walked upstairs and I cried for hours because this town was kind enough to care about me."

"For me it was day one," Rachel said quietly. "I was on my last ten dollars and I blew out a tire at the base of the mountain. Mel found me and I didn't have a spare so he brought me to Stella's and arranged to have one sent down and put on my crappy car. By the time I knew what was happening, I had a job and food in my belly and I was home. I sat down in that café and I cried for an hour. I was so worried Stella would tell me she'd made a terrible mistake, but she just patted my hand and told me everyone who comes to Bliss breaks down at some point. She said it was because Bliss was the place to go when you had nowhere else. Bliss is the end of the line, the place where you decide to stop running from your problems and face them so you can start living again."

Face them. Look at her problems because she wasn't alone with them. She hadn't been alone in Dallas, but somehow it was easier here. "I can't have any more babies."

Two hands squeezed hers.

"I'm so sorry to hear that," they murmured. No one told her she should be happy with the ones she had. They seemed to know she was, but allowed her to mourn what she'd lost.

"We didn't plan," she said haltingly, getting to the heart of the problem. "We didn't think we had to. We wanted nature to take its course and…"

Callie leaned in. "What do you mean?"

"I think both my kids are Adam's and Jake is going to feel so betrayed when he realizes I didn't give him a child." There it was. Out in the open, the ghost that had been haunting her.

Callie's eyes went wide. "Did you talk about it? Did they want to make sure?"

She shook her head. "We thought we had all the time in the world. We wanted four or five kids, so we didn't do DNA tests or make sure one of them wore a condom so they each had a child of their blood."

Callie's hand went over hers, over Jen's and Nell's, and she was surrounded by feminine caring. "There is no blood. Not in this kind of relationship. There's only found family, and it's so important that blood doesn't matter. We have talked about it, Nate and Zane and I. The first pregnancy was hard on me. I don't know if I want another one."

Rachel's eyes went wide. "Callie? Are you sure?"

She shook her head. "Not at all. I know I want to wait, and that means every year that goes by hurts our chances. Not once has Zane complained that he didn't get his kid. Do you know why?"

Tears streamed down her face because she was looking at everything from her standpoint and not theirs. She was viewing herself as some thing they always got an equal piece of or they behaved like children who couldn't share a toy, and that so was not her men. She wasn't giving them credit, wasn't giving them the chance to comfort her and to talk about what was wrong because she pretended like there wasn't anything. She was holding back.

"Because I already have two kids, baby," a deep voice said. "I don't need more. I'll take them. If you change your mind, I'll take any child we have. Hell, if we find one somewhere, I'll take that one, too. Who knows? It's Bliss. Weird shit happens here." Zane Hollister was standing at their table, his beautiful face solemn. "Ms. Dean-Miles, I don't know your husbands, but I know the kind of men who need the relationship you're in. They aren't selfish. They care more about the love they've found than any traditional child you could give them. And they love their wives more than anything. They love her so much, they're willing to share her. And their children are theirs no matter who they look like. Charlie and Zander are ours and I'm their dad no matter whose DNA was used to make them. My love will be imprinted on them and that's what counts. But you won't believe it until you hear it from them."

She had to talk to them, especially Jake. She wasn't sure, but neither child looked like Jake and she would bet her life Tristan was Adam's.

"Let me take you out to the Movie Motel and you can call them on the landline," Callie said. "When you're done you can either be alone or we can watch the movie of the night and eat lemon pie, if you feel like company."

"It's *Harry Potter*," Jen said.

Lemon pie and *Harry Potter*. Some things were different and others so close to home.

"Yes, I think I would like that."

Twenty minutes later, she was alone, her new friends sitting in lawn chairs and watching Harry meet Ron and Hermione.

She picked up the phone and dialed, her hand shaking.

"Baby?" Jake's voice came over the line, his worry apparent in his tone. "Serena, baby, are you all right? I got your message and we've been going insane. What do you mean you got arrested? I can have Mitch there in the morning."

"Calm down, Jake." She hadn't meant to scare them. "I'm fine. I'm… Jake…"

His voice lost the panic. "Baby… Serena, talk to me. Tell me what's happening. Fuck. I know what's happening, but I can't talk about it until you do. I can't… I just want you to know how much I love you and our kids. We're complete, Serena. You and me and Adam and our kids. We're whole. There's nothing missing. Nothing else I would want."

"You knew?"

"I knew the hysterectomy bothered you."

"What if…"

"What if what? What if neither of those babies I love so fucking much don't have a drop of my DNA?" Jake asked softly. "I was there when they were conceived and if that's true then they're the combination of the two people I love most in this world, and that means everything to me. I don't say it to him because it's not physical between us, but I love Adam. He's one-third of my soul. One-fifth, because our kids took their part, too, and I don't want it back. I want those pieces of me held in the people I love most, and dear god, I need my wife to know how grateful I am with the family she gave me. You made us a family, Serena. I don't need some uterus to make me love you. We don't need more. We need this. Us. You and Adam and our kids, baby, you aren't just enough. You are my whole world."

She sobbed as his words finally broke through to her.

"What's happening? Is that Serena?" Adam's voice was saying over the line.

"She's fine. Our wife is fine," Jake said, his voice patient, but she could hear the emotion behind it. "She's perfect and when she comes home to us, we're going to prove it to her."

He loved her. It was enough. "I'm sorry I've been so distant."

"No, baby. You needed time, but never think that I wasn't going to be right here waiting for you because I was merely waiting for you to come home to us."

Waiting. They'd been waiting and she'd felt alone. She should have known that she was never alone. Not with two husbands who loved her, who understood her.

Who would never let her go too far away.

She cried and knew no matter what came her way, she wasn't alone.

Serena opened the door to the Movie Motel, surprised to see Nell standing there. It was ten in the morning and she wasn't due to leave until this afternoon. She'd managed to change her flight and Zane Hollister had offered to drive her to the airport and take care of her rental when it was ready to go back. She was meeting Callie and the others for lunch in a couple of hours.

She was seriously thinking of buying a cabin here. It would be good for her kiddos to see they weren't the only ones in the world with two dads.

"Hi, Nell. How are you?"

"I was wondering the same about you," Nell said. "I was hoping I could show you this place I know. I realize that you called your husbands last night and worked things out with them, but there's another layer I think you're neglecting."

"What's that?"

Nell held a hand out, her face solemn. "I know that every time I lost a baby I would feel...like less of a woman. Let me take you somewhere amazing. Somewhere you'll know how special your body is no matter what you've lost."

Damn it. She wasn't through crying yet. She took Nell's hand and let her lead the way.

Was she doing this? She was totally doing this. She was on a mountain and she was naked and she was going to walk outside with all the other naked people.

Nell had driven her up to a place called the Mountain and Valley Naturist Community. She'd promised it was a magical place.

"It's okay," Nell said, not seeming to care that she was totally naked and about to walk outside. "Think of it like a club for people who don't get the spanking thing. Not any kinder, but a little gentler. Walk outside. Feel the sun on your skin and let it make you feel young and vital. Let it remind you that you're alive and whole and loved."

The woman had a way with words.

Serena stepped into the sunlight and let it hit her skin, felt the grass beneath her toes, and heard the soothing chatter of people all around her. She lifted her face to the sun.

She was alive and whole and loved. It was enough.

"Now that is a beautiful woman," a familiar voice said.

"The most beautiful woman," another agreed.

She opened her eyes and Adam and Jake were standing there, gloriously naked.

"This place really is magic," Nell whispered. "But there's no magic quite like a happily ever after. I called them yesterday and told them they should come up here for a few days. You're booked in a suite. Enjoy your men, Serena. Welcome to Bliss."

Serena ran to them and as their arms surrounded her, she knew she was whole again.

- Hot Ham & Cheese Rolls
- Wild Rice Dressing with Sausage & Cranberries
- Slow Cooker Chicken & Dumplings
- Slow Cooker Honey Soy Pot Roast
- Easy Breakfast Casserole
- Banana Pudding
- Peach Cobbler
- Key Lime Cake
- Spiked Strawberry Lemonade

Slice of Life
Damon and Penny in "She's the Boss"

Women of McKay-Taggart
The Long Wait

Hot Ham & Cheese Rolls

12 Hawaiian dinner rolls

1/2 cup mayonnaise

1 (8 ounce) package thinly sliced deli ham

6-8 slices Swiss cheese

2 tablespoons Dijon mustard

4 tablespoons butter, melted

1 tablespoon poppy seeds

1 teaspoon Worcestershire sauce

Preheat oven to 350 degrees. Cut rolls in half and spread each side with mayonnaise. Place a slice of ham and cheese on one side of each roll. Place the remaining half of the rolls on top of the ham and cheese and place in a large baking dish, making sure they are close together. In a small bowl, combine the mustard, butter, poppy seeds and Worcestershire sauce and pour over the top of the rolls. Cover with foil and bake for 10 minutes. Uncover and bake for an additional 2-3 minutes, or until tops are browned.

Wild Rice Dressing with Sausage & Cranberries

1 BOX WILD RICE

1 STICK BUTTER

1 CELERY STALK, CHOPPED (1/2 CUP)

½ CUP SWEET ONION, CHOPPED

1 POUND SAGE SAUSAGE, COOKED AND CRUMBLED

1 CUP DRIED CRANBERRIES

½ CUP PECANS, CHOPPED

Cook wild rice per package directions and set aside. In a small skillet, over medium heat, melt butter and sauté celery and onion for 8-10 minutes. In a large bowl, add the wild rice, sausage, celery, onion, cranberries and pecans. Stir to combine and serve on a large platter.

Slow Cooker Chicken & Dumplings

4-6 BONELESS, SKINLESS CHICKEN BREASTS

1 TEASPOON CHICKEN BOUILLON

1 TEASPOON PEPPER

1 CAN CREAM OF CHICKEN SOUP

1 CAN CREAM OF CELERY SOUP

2 CANS CHICKEN BROTH

1 (16 OUNCE) BAG FROZEN PEAS AND CARROTS

1 CAN REFRIGERATED BISCUITS

Place chicken in slow cooker. Sprinkle with chicken bouillon and pepper. Mix together the soup and broth. Pour over chicken, cover and cook on low 6 hours. Shred chicken, using 2 forks. Stir in peas and carrots. Increase heat setting to high and allow to cook while preparing dumplings. Roll biscuits to flatten to 1/4-inch thickness. Cut each biscuit into 4 strips. Place strips in stew, pressing gently with back of spoon to submerge in liquid. Cover. Cook on high for 1 ½ hours, or until dumplings are thoroughly cooked.

Slow Cooker Honey Soy Pot Roast

4-5 POUND CHUCK ROAST

1 CUP FLOUR

SALT AND PEPPER TO TASTE

1/4 CUP OIL

1 VIDALIA ONION, THINLY SLICED

2 TABLESPOONS MINCED GARLIC

1/4 CUP SOY SAUCE

1 CAN BEEF BROTH

1/2 CUP WHITE WINE

1/4 CUP HONEY

1 TABLESPOON SAGE

Cover roast in flour and sprinkle with salt and pepper. Heat oil in skillet on medium high heat and sear roast on all sides. Place in slow cooker. In a medium bowl, combine remaining ingredients and pour over roast. Cook on low for 8 hours. Serve over white rice.

Easy Breakfast Casserole

- 6 SLICES SANDWICH BREAD (WHITE IS BEST)
- 1 POUND BULK SAUSAGE, COOKED AND DRAINED (CUBED HAM MAY BE SUBSTITUTED)
- 2 CUPS SHARP CHEDDAR CHEESE, GRATED
- 1 BUNCH GREEN ONION, CHOPPED (OPTIONAL)
- 1 (4 OUNCE) CAN MUSHROOMS (OPTIONAL)
- 1 DOZEN EGGS
- ½ CUP MILK
- SALT AND PEPPER TO TASTE

Cube bread and place in the bottom of a greased 9 x 13-inch casserole dish. Cover with meat and cheese (if you choose to add onion and mushrooms, add now). Mix together the eggs and milk and pour over casserole. Cover and refrigerate overnight. Wake up and put in oven at 350 degrees for 1 hour. Serve hot.

Slice of Life

DAMON AND PENNY IN "SHE'S THE BOSS"

GIRLS NIGHT

Penelope Knight smiled at her giggling boy. This morning he was staring at her like she was an angel looking down at him, though he'd quite played the devil the night before. Ear infection, the doctor had pronounced. She'd spent much of the night walking the floor with him and it showed on her face this morning.

Not that she hadn't worked on too little sleep before, but in the beginning it had been because Damon wouldn't let her rest. When they'd first married, he'd been on top of her every chance he'd gotten, and a few he'd artificially invented. Then their son had come. He was the light of her life, but sometimes she worried she was more mother than wife now.

"At least one of us is awake." Damon stepped in behind her, one arm around her as he reached down and put his hand on their son. Such a big hand. Despite the fact that Ollie was toddling around, his father's hand still covered most of his torso. "I hope you're feeling better, son."

"I think the antibiotic started working around three or so," she said, covering a yawn.

Damon kissed her forehead and stepped back, looking entirely too perfect in his tailored suit. The man always took her breath away. Six foot three, with midnight dark hair that was only slightly going silver at the temples. It made him look distinguished, stately, quite like the boss he was. "I wish you would have woken me and let me take my turn."

"You have twenty interviews today." She'd known when Ollie had been so fussy the night before that she wouldn't wake her husband. It was far easier for her to take the day off. Her job at McKay-Taggart and Knight was a flexible one, and she liked it that way. She was there if they needed her translation skills. She'd managed to break several codes even while rocking her son to sleep.

It was a good life, but she missed her husband in the last few months. It wasn't like Damon was gone or had distanced himself from her. He was right there beside her, holding her hand and relying on her. But they were new parents and this was what happened, according to her sister. Diana—who should know because she had three children herself—had told Penny she would know when the time had come.

One of you will break, probably Damon. He'll stop everything and give you a look you won't be able to say no to, and it will be fast and furious and so good because it's been so long and you'll know that you're going to make it. You'll have solid proof that loving your child doesn't make you less of a woman but more of one. Don't worry, sister. It will happen and soon.

He stared down at her, his gray eyes warm. "It's more like six interviews, and I would send them all away if it meant you got some sleep, love." His hands cupped her face. "You have to know that."

She did and that was precisely why it was incredibly easy to sacrifice her sleep for his. She went up on her toes and brushed her mouth over his. "I do, but I also know that we need another female operative. We've put it off and put it off, but it's time now, Damon. With Kayla on a long-term assignment, we don't have anyone."

He pulled her into his arms. "We have you."

"I'm not a femme fatale," she replied. "And you would have a bloody heart attack if I went into the field anyway."

He sighed, holding on to her. "You are perfectly fatal to me, love. More woman than I could have hoped for, and you're right. You're not going into the field. We're a happy old Mum and Dad. I'll find some young, adventurous thing to do the dirty work and we can stay at home and put our feet up by the fire. We've put in our time."

Well, he certainly had. Damon had been one of MI6's most dangerous agents. She'd gone into the field exactly once—with him. It was enough. It had been the adventure of a lifetime.

She kissed him again. "We certainly have. So go find us another Kay. I worry that actor she's working with is going to steal her away from us, and we desperately need some women around here. I adore the lads, you know, but..."

He stepped back, putting his hands up. "Say no more. It's like having a pack of overly curious puppies at one's feet at all times. And they're not housetrained. I swear Big Tag knew exactly what he was doing when he left that group here. He was punishing me."

The Lost Boys were six men the team had found when they'd taken down Hope McDonald's evil experiments. Well, five of them were. The sixth was Owen, their friend and colleague. He'd been McDonald's last victim, and knowing he would likely never remember the first thirty-five years of his life hurt. "I think Ian was simply trying to protect them all."

Damon backed up, smoothing down his jacket as he went. "Tucker put a bath bomb in the loo. The damn thing overflowed the toilet and we had glitter everywhere. Who puts glitter in their bath? They're all lunatics, I tell you." His eyes softened. "See you for lunch? Unless you're tired, and then I understand."

Yes, he would. He understood and she understood, and it was all lovely, but she missed the times when he didn't understand. When he had to have her and nothing else would matter.

"I'll see you for lunch. I love you, Damon Knight."

"Not as much as I love you, Penelope Knight."

She watched as he strode out the door. Her own James Bond.

The baby cried out as though he could only handle not being the center of attention for so long. She reached down and picked him up, cuddling her boy close.

It was enough for now.

An hour later, Penny made her way down to the office section of The Garden. She and Damon talked about moving, finding a place in the country where they would have some more privacy, but she rather liked the community that came with living in The Garden. It was fun to walk out of her flat and know that everyone in the building was a friend.

"Morning, Mrs. Knight," Owen said, tipping his head as he passed her in the hall. He was wearing a pair of sweats and a T-shirt, obviously heading down to the gym after refilling his water bottle.

"Good morning, Owen." She kept trying to get him to use her first name, to be more like the friendly, flirty Scot they'd lost. "How are you today?"

He grinned, a devastating expression. The man was gorgeous. "The dining room is full of lovely ladies. Do you think Damon needs any help with the interviews?"

Ah, there he was. Sometimes now he seemed serious and dark, and other times she could see the man he'd been. She smiled back. "Somehow I think you and Damon would have different priorities when it comes to female operatives."

Tucker strode out of the gym, his eyes wide. "Owen, dude, I heard the dining room is filled with women and we should go pick one."

Good lord. Tucker would frighten them away. Or one of them would try to adopt the lad. "They are not prostitutes, Tucker. They're merely women here looking for a job."

Tucker frowned. "But I'm told dealing with me is a job. Everyone says it."

Owen put a hand on his shoulder and started leading him back to the gym.

The lads did take care of each other. She sighed and moved into the dining room. She needed caffeine to get through the day. She stepped inside amid the clatter of coffee cups.

It wasn't completely full. There were only a few women in the room. Six, but they were all quite lovely. They'd been recommended by either Ian Taggart or their old boss at MI6, Nigel Crowe. They had all passed strict security tests. Every single one would be educated, physically fit, deadly.

Young. Beautiful. Toned and fit.

Two of the six were sitting by themselves, at separate tables. One was brunette, the other a lovely auburn-haired woman. She had her tablet out, studying whatever was on the screen. Four of the women were clustered around the coffeemaker, talking quietly. They were in the poshest of clothing, each designer suit or sheath molding to their taut bodies. God, there wasn't one in the lot who looked like she was out of her twenties.

It didn't matter. She trusted Damon would find someone who would fit in. Kayla was a vibrant light to the group. Without her they were missing something essential.

Penny smiled as the auburn-haired woman looked up and nodded her way.

"No one's sitting here if you need a place to wait," she said, offering up a chair. "I hear we could be here for a while. The boss of this place is apparently very thorough."

It was good Damon had a reputation. "No, thank you. I'm not applying for the job. Just grabbing a cuppa."

She moved on, wondering what these women specialized in. They would all be deadly, but some would know different parts of the security and intelligence world better than the others. Perhaps one of these women would become a new friend. She was looking forward to meeting whoever Damon selected.

"Of course. Do you work here?"

"I do," she replied quietly, not wanting to disturb the brunette, who seemed deeply invested in the computer in front of her. "Don't be intimidated by Damon. He's a big teddy bear."

A lovely smile crossed the other woman's face. "I'm sure he is to his family, but that man won the Victoria Cross. He's a legend and a hero. I'm all right being intimidated by him. I'm simply thrilled to be able to meet him. I hope I can get to the point where I meet his team. His wife is a legend, too."

Penny smiled. At least the woman had done her homework. "I don't know about that. Good luck on your interview."

She moved to the coffeemaker. Some caffeine and a bit of sugar and she would be ready for the day.

"That man is gorgeous and he's got some kinks, if you know what I mean," a woman with raven hair was saying, her accent giving away her country of origin. French. Parisian, to be exact. Well educated, almost certainly from the upper classes. She spoke English with ease and likely could speak it without an accent when she wanted to.

"I should think so," a woman with a flat Midwestern-American accent said. Also well educated, but Penny had studied languages and accents for so long she could hear the rural underpinnings to the woman's speech. "When I was shown in, at first I thought all the plants were for show, but I caught the weird sex stuff behind some of them. I think the rumors were right. Knight is a lot like Taggart, and not just in the professional sense."

Penny slowed down, not able to help listening in. It wasn't like they hid their lifestyle, and Taggart wouldn't have sent anyone who couldn't tolerate a bit of D/s. Still, it was good to hear what the newbies thought without Damon around.

She didn't feel bad about it. They were being quite open and she was, after all, a spy in the middle of a group of professionals. Shouldn't they be a bit more discreet?

"I only want the job so I can get into the club," a woman with a London accent said. "Honestly, I hate field work, but The Garden is legendary. I want to get in, find a Dom, and then let the bastard take care of me before this job gets me shot."

Well, that was nice to know. She was certainly going to tell Damon to cross that one off the list.

She reached for the coffeepot.

"I know which Dom I want," the raven-haired beauty said. "I think I'll take the boss."

London accent shook her head. "He's married."

Paris waved a hand. "I've heard she's an old hag of a woman and he only married her out of pity. She saved his life on a mission. Everyone knows he hides her away here because he's embarrassed."

Midwest shook her head. "I heard he married her because Taggart wanted a married man in the position, and given his heart condition, Knight couldn't get another job. He picked the first woman he saw and he'll probably divorce her when he finds a more suitable wife."

Paris smoothed her hair down. "Well, I intend to be that woman. At least to see if he's as good in bed as he looks. We'll take it from there and see if he's husband material."

"I wouldn't mind meeting a Taggart," Midwest said. "I saw the youngest with his wife once and she wasn't anything to look at."

Penny rather thought Erin was lovely, but she wasn't in a conventional way. Of course, there was one problem with all of that. "If you think you're going after one of the Taggart men, you should probably think again."

Paris put a hand on her hip. "I don't believe we invited you to join this conversation." She looked Penny up and down and obviously found her wanting. "If you're here for the job… You can't be here for the job. You aren't even dressed for a janitorial job, much less one with a man like Knight. What on earth is on your shirt? It's disgusting. *T'es sale. Personne te prendra sérieusement.*"

Penny looked down at her shirt. Sure enough, there was a stain on it. She'd been feeding her son and he'd grabbed her at some point. There was always some part of her stained with milk or baby food or spit up.

Damon usually had some on him as well.

She waited for the old insecurities to well up, waited for the urge to run and hide away and cry.

Not a single one of those instincts surged to the forefront. She wanted coffee. That was the only disturbing part. She wanted coffee and they were in her bloody way.

Well, there was also a bit of unholy rage that these women were thinking of screwing her husband, but she did understand it a bit. He was gorgeous and fuckable. He was also hers.

He was hers to love and fuck and raise a family with. He'd chosen her, and for absolutely none of the reasons these women had specified.

"Hey, not everyone speaks French, you know." The auburn-haired woman had stood up. "If you want to bully someone, why don't you come over here and see how it goes?"

Oh, she liked that one. It was too easy to not stand up to the mean girls. Even in their business there was still all that societal training and the need to fly under the radar.

Paris looked her over. "I know who you are, *pute*. Do you honestly believe you're going to get hired on after sleeping with a client who turned on you? And the one over there is an idiot. Her husband worked for the cartels for years and it got past her. Well, some of us think she was probably in on it, but we'll never know, will we? I have no idea why Knight would even call you in for an interview."

Ah, now she knew who they were. She'd read files on all of the candidates, discussing each with Damon. The quiet brunette Paris was referring to was a woman named Carmen Vega. Her husband had been a double and she'd been forced to kill him before he killed her. She'd left the CIA shortly after, but Taggart felt she was solid. The auburn-haired lady was Nina Blunt. She'd worked with Interpol for years until they'd fired her for falling in love with a man who was using her for intelligence.

Carmen stood up. "I would say you're the idiot here, Merlyn, if you don't know who you're talking to." She turned to the lady with the Midwestern accent. "And you're too stupid to be here if you're thinking about hitting on Theo Taggart."

Penny couldn't help but smile at the thought. Erin would love it so much. It had probably been entirely too long since she'd been allowed to murder someone. "Please do. I'll give you his mobile number. You could send him a picture or something."

Carmen snorted, but somehow made it sound elegant. "You're mean."

Paris looked down her nose at Penny. "I think it's time you left. I don't care whose secretary you are, I doubt Knight allows you to talk to his operatives like this."

Carmen's eyes had lit with intent. "Do you want me to handle this, boss? I will admit I'm carrying two weapons, but I don't need either of them to take care of that one. She's all desk job."

Paris put her hands on her nonexistent hips. "How dare you?"

But Penny was more concerned with what else the operative had dared. "I thought Damon said no weapons allowed."

Nina flushed, too. "Sorry. I have a semi on me. Your security isn't as good as you think. You're relying on metal detectors and I had mine made from a 3-D printer. It's comprised of thermoplastics so I can really only get one shot off with it, but it will get through metal detectors and it can come in handy."

Oh, those two were definitely interesting.

The door to the dining room opened and Damon stepped inside, holding a file folder in his hand. "Merlyn Fabrice?"

Every woman in the room turned to him.

Penelope was fairly certain he couldn't see her since Nina had stepped in front of her, as though the woman worried Paris might attack. Naturally, the woman was much taller. It could be difficult to always be the shortest person in a room.

"That is me, Mr. Knight." Paris's stilettos clicked along the floor. "*Bonjour.* I have to say you have a few very rude employees. I hope they're not all like this one."

"This one?" Damon asked.

"Wow, she is not smart," Carmen said under her breath.

Penny popped out from behind Nina, giving her husband a brilliant smile. It was then she caught what she must have missed before. He'd slipped out of his jacket and there was a small handprint on his right shoulder. He must have missed it. It was faintly green. She'd fed Ollie a mix of bananas and avocados—a mix that sounded disgusting but was quite nice. At some point he'd picked up their son and held him close and then slipped on his jacket, covering the imperfection.

Penny stopped because this was it. Oh, this was it. He was standing there, his hand on Paris's perfectly manicured one, and heat flooded Penny's body. She'd been too tired, too overwhelmed, but now pure lust flooded her system. Damon was the most gorgeous man she'd ever seen, and she loved every inch of his scarred body, and she loved the fact that their son's paw print was on that perfectly pressed shirt of his.

Penny stepped up. "I'm afraid she's talking about me, Damon."

One brow rose over Damon's eyes and he dropped Paris's hand. She knew her husband and saw the second he caught the heat coming off her. "She's talking about you, Penelope? What did you do?"

Yes, he'd gotten her quite nicely. His voice had gone low and deep, his eyes locking on hers.

"As I said, she's quite rude and she eavesdrops, not something you want your…staff to be doing," Paris said, staring back at Penny. "I'm afraid we should talk about that in your office. I can help you with staff. You're far too busy a man to have to deal with low-level employees."

"You've been eavesdropping?" Damon asked, his lips curling faintly.

"Undoubtedly," she replied. Oh, she rather hoped no one noticed how hard her nipples had gotten the minute Damon turned those predatory eyes of his on her. He was looking at her like a starving man and she was his feast.

It was going to be everything Diana had told her—fast and furious and so very satisfying.

And then perhaps it could be slow and long. She was ready. How could she not be when he was looking at her like that? It was so odd how insecure she'd been when she was younger and more perfect. Somehow the scars and fine lines of her body had come with a newfound confidence.

He loved her curves and her scars and how her face was changing—though she wasn't sure he would ever see it.

That man's lust and love was the best anti-aging plan she could ever have.

"So you've been listening in and likely making some assessments. And have you come to some conclusions, Mrs. Knight? Help me out, love. I have other things I'd rather do this afternoon," he replied.

Like her. Yes, she knew that man's language quite well. "I think I can handle this one, Damon." She looked at Paris. "Ms. Fabrice, we won't be hiring you. Please remove yourself from my presence or you'll upset my husband when he figures out exactly how you've disrespected me."

"Excuse me?" Damon seemed to have grown a few inches, his gaze swinging around to the woman Penny had mentioned.

Paris stepped away from him.

Penny moved between the women and her husband. More for their sake than his. "Don't worry about it. I don't care what someone I don't know thinks of me. We won't be hiring those three either, but I intend to put Carmen Vega and Nina Blunt on the payroll. They'll be lovely operatives and will fit in quite well with our group."

Paris huffed. "You can't make those kinds of decisions."

Damon's hand slipped into hers. "I assure you, she can. I might have the big desk, but she's been the boss since the day she took me in hand. Carmen and Nina, please let Teresa at the front desk know my wife has hired you both and to get your paperwork started. I'll have Nick give you a tour of the building. The rest of you should leave before I'm less distracted by my gorgeous wife and figure out exactly what you did or said that might have upset me. Note I didn't say her. She wouldn't be upset because she's quite above that. I am not. Go."

Those women proved they could run in heels.

Nina started to walk forward. "Mr. Knight…"

Carmen put a hand on her arm. "Nope, the boss is about to run out of here and we won't see him for a bit." She smiled wistfully. "I remember that feeling. We'll be fine on our own."

Damon leaned over and swept her off her feet once again. "Excellent choices, my love."

Nothing in the world felt better than Damon carrying her along like she weighed nothing at all. "I'm good at handling employees. Let me show you how good I am at handling you."

He kicked open the door to his office. "There was never a doubt to that." He set her on her feet and sank his hands in her hair, staring at her like he was seeing her for the first time. "I love you, Penelope Knight. Don't forget it for a single moment. I'm here because you love me. I'm whole because of you."

Every word he said lifted her up.

"I'm here because of you. I have everything I ever wanted because of you, Damon. Let's show each other just what we need. If we can't make love at night, I want to do it in the afternoon, in the morning, whenever we have a chance, I want to be in your arms," she said.

"In my mind, you're never out of them." He kissed her, pulling her close and letting her feel how much he wanted her.

When he came up for air, Penny stepped away. "Hold that thought. And you were wrong about something you said this morning."

His hand went to his tie, pulling it off. "What was I wrong about?"

"You said we'd had the adventure of a lifetime when were on the Royale," she pointed out. "But you were wrong. This is our adventure, Damon. And it will last a lifetime."

She moved to the door, closing it and locking the world away for a while.

Banana Pudding

2 PACKAGES VANILLA FLAVORED INSTANT PUDDING

3 CUPS MILK

1 BOX VANILLA WAFERS

2-3 BANANAS, SLICED

2 CONTAINERS WHIPPED TOPPING

Using a hand mixer, beat pudding and milk together for 2-3 minutes. Let stand for 5 minutes. In a trifle bowl, arrange 1/3 of the vanilla wafers on the bottom and top with 1/3 pudding, 1/3 bananas and 1/3 whipped topping. Repeat layers 2 more times, ending with whipped topping. Refrigerate for at least 3 hours before serving.

Peach Cobbler

2 (15.25 OUNCE) CANS PEACHES IN HEAVY SYRUP

1 BOX YELLOW CAKE MIX

1 STICK BUTTER, MELTED

1 TEASPOON CINNAMON

Preheat oven to 375 degrees. Pour peaches in a 9 x 13-inch baking dish. Cover the peaches with the cake mix, mixing gently to cover. Pour butter over entire dish and bake for 45 minutes. Serve with vanilla ice cream.

Key Lime Cake

1 PACKAGE LEMON CAKE MIX

1 1/3 CUP OIL

4 EGGS

1 (3 OUNCE) PACKAGE LIME FLAVORED JELL-O

¾ CUP ORANGE JUICE

Combine all ingredients and mix well. Pour into three 8-inch cake pans or a 12-cup standard muffin tin. Bake according to instructions on box. Allow to cool, then frost with cream cheese icing. For the cake, spread the icing between the layers and on the top and sides of the cake.

Cream Cheese Icing

1 (8 OUNCE) PACKAGE CREAM CHEESE

1 STICK BUTTER, SOFTENED

1 TEASPOON VANILLA

4 CUPS CONFECTIONER'S SUGAR

In a stand mixer, beat together the cream cheese, butter and vanilla. Slowly add the sugar and beat on low until blended.

Spiked Strawberry Lemonade

MAKES A 2 LITER PITCHER

1 CAN FROZEN STRAWBERRY DAIQUIRI CONCENTRATE, THAWED

1 CAN FROZEN LEMONADE, THAWED

4 CUPS LEMON LIME SODA

2 CUPS VODKA

Combine all ingredients and refrigerate for 2 hours before serving.

Women of McKay-Taggart

THE LONG WAIT

Charlotte

Charlie pulled up to Serena's, expertly negotiating her Lincoln Navigator into the long driveway. It was easy to park today since Jake's massive SUV wasn't here. It was in the parking lot at McKay-Taggart and had been for hours.

It would stay there until Jake and Adam were through with the mission and went to pick it up. Just like Ian's F-150 would be safe in the confines of the parking garage. All those spaces were taken up right now, but they would be empty later because everyone would be safe and come home.

Positivity. That was what a day like this called for.

The door to the main house opened and Serena rushed outside. Like she'd been sitting there waiting, and she probably had.

"Have you heard anything yet?" Serena asked. Her voice was steady, but there was no way to miss the tension in her body.

How many times had she and Serena gone through this together? Ten? Twenty? It was hard to remember them all. Some of the group needed to be alone for the wait, but Serena couldn't handle it so at the very least Charlotte and Avery always made their way over to her place or invited her to theirs. They would sit and talk. They would drink when they could and help with each other's kiddos. They would hold on to each other when the worry got to be too much.

This was the sisterhood.

Before she could get out, Serena had the car door open and was helping the kids climb down. Kenzie and Kala went straight into Serena's arms.

"Daddy's working," Kala said solemnly.

Daddy worked every day, but somehow the words seemed wise, as though her tiny daughter understood there was a difference when Daddy went to work at odd hours and Momma took off for her aunties' homes or they showed up at hers.

"I know, baby," Serena replied, ruffling Kala's hair gently. "Uncle Adam and Uncle Jake are working, too. It's going to be okay because they're going to finish their work and join us here for the party. They won't let us down, baby girl. They'll be here. Let's go inside and start getting ready. Tristan has some snacks. Do you want some?"

Kenzie brightened up but Kala merely gave her a slow nod, as though she'd thought it through and it was all right to snack. Eating wouldn't change the situation for the better or the worse, so she was okay with it.

Her babies. So like her and Ian. Kenzie was impulsive and threw herself into life with zest. Kala was careful, thinking through her every move.

Serena set them down and pointed to the door. "Go on then. You know the way. Your Aunt Mia is in the back with the kids."

When the girls were through the door, she turned back to Charlie, who was gently lifting up her sleeping son's car seat.

"Any news?"

Charlie shook her head. "It could be hours. I know they managed to infiltrate the building with no problems, but they can't simply go after the Ukrainians. They're only part of the problem. The real problem is de Vries. They know he's coming to meet the Ukrainians and make the trade—Steph for Anya. They don't know when that meeting is taking place. Until then, they're all in place and waiting."

The Ukrainians had shown up the night before at Sanctum of all places, proving they had their own good intel. A mercenary group was after Dr. Stephanie Gibson and they had unfortunately taken Steph's friend and nurse Anya Shadrova as a hostage. Her brother was a member of the Ukrainian mob and wanted his sister back. He wasn't planning on playing fair.

But then her husband was cool with unfair, too. That was precisely why he and a whole group of deadly ex-Special Forces operatives were currently lying in wait.

It was the end of the op, she hoped. Ezra Fain had been called in so the CIA would be backing the MT team up. She prayed.

Because they were going up against some very bad men with lots of guns. They would be outnumbered. Anything could go wrong. God, hadn't Theo taught them that?

She took a deep breath. It wouldn't go wrong. It would be fine because they were the best.

Her husband and brothers-in-law and brothers-of-the-heart and Erin would be fine. They would do their job and get Steph and Tucker back. They might kill Alfi, but she was okay with that.

The point was everything would be fine, and she and Serena and Avery would get ready for Jake's birthday barbecue. They would have a lot to celebrate, and when the guys got here, they would be hungry and thirsty.

"Are you okay?" Serena asked.

She forced a smile on her face. "Of course. Ian's fine. I know he is. I trust him."

"I didn't mean that. I trust him, too. I meant it has to be hard for you. Avery and I never think twice. We wouldn't go out in the field, but you've been there. You're as good a shot as Erin. You've had a ton of training."

She shook her head. "Not the way the others have. I wasn't trained to function as part of a team."

She'd been trained to work alone, to be deadly as any venomous snake. To strike hard and fast.

How far she'd come from that world.

"But you want to be the one to back him up," Serena continued.

Of course she did. She wanted to be right there beside her husband, making damn sure no one got the drop on him. She wanted to be there, ready to give him anything he might need. That was her job.

Unfortunately, it wasn't her only job.

"We made a promise when we had kids that one of us would stay out of harm's way," she replied quietly. "Honestly, since the girls came along, Ian only goes into the field when he has to. He knows he's moving into a more managerial role with the team and he's usually good with it."

But he missed the field. She could see it in his eyes. He'd been eager for this. The minute they'd figured out why Tucker had allowed himself to be taken, Ian had clapped his hands together, his eyes filled with a fierce light.

It would be all right. Ian was surrounded by people who would take care of him. He and Li and Alex would stick together. His brothers and Erin were backing him up, and they'd taken the whole bodyguard crew with them. Brody was the one she should worry about. Brody was the one who would be emotional.

The big Aussie had kissed his son and walked away because he had to try to save Nate's mother.

"How's Nate?"

Serena had taken him home with her. Avery had gone along, staying what was left of the night here with Serena.

Serena smiled and picked up the bag Charlie had brought. "That kid can eat. He's a sweetie. He's fascinated by the other kids. Aidan and Tristan have been amusing him, but I think he's been waiting for the girls."

Her girls were charmers when it came to babies. Or outcasts. They were pretty good at figuring out which kids were getting the short end of the social stick and dealing with the jerks giving it to them. She feared for their junior high years. And was also totally excited about them.

"Erin and Theo dropped TJ off before they joined the others," Avery explained. "It's kid central back there. Mia stayed with us last night, too. She's in the back with the babies."

All the Taggart wives got together when trouble came their way. She was sure at some point in time Sean and Grace would show up to see if they could help.

Charlotte's phone buzzed and a momentary flare of panic went through her. She forced herself to stay calm. It was just a text. No one would send her bad news in a text. They had protocols. A text was merely an update. She reached into her pocket as she followed Serena into the house.

"Anyone else getting a text?" Charlie asked.

Avery was standing in the kitchen, pouring mugs of coffee. She glanced down at the counter where her phone sat. "Nope."

Serena shook her head. "Not me."

Good. Bad news tended to run rampant. She set Seth down and swiped her phone to read the text.

Hey, baby. Can you send a copy of "Welcome to the Jungle" to my phone? I don't know how I lost it, but it's not here and I need a theme song. You know how important that is. Love you.

She could send him an audio file. Easy peasy. She texted him back.

Sure thing, babe. One theme song coming your way.

"You need some coffee?" Avery offered. "We've got the menu ready, but there's a ton of prep work."

Being in the kitchen would be good for her soul. It was easy, busy work. Avery was the one who could really cook, and Charlie would happily chop anything Avery put in front of her. She was good with a knife. She would totally pretend she was chopping up asshat Dutch mercenaries. Or Ukrainian mobsters who just had to stick their noses in everything. "Thanks. I can definitely use the coffee. We didn't get home until almost dawn. By we I mean me and three small children. I have no idea how single moms manage. How my mom managed. Just getting them to bed was a Herculean task. Sometimes I wish I could attach a basket to Bud and let him carry a couple in from the car. I hate leaving them alone even in the garage."

She logged into her media account. She shared one with Ian, but as hers was also filled with songs about bouncing lollipops and lost dogs finding their way home, they kept separate lists. She had to figure out how to move the song from her list to his. How hard could that be?

She couldn't drag it over to his. The screen was too small. She was trying to use the app instead of the full software and she rarely even tried to use it for anything except to play music from her phone. The damn screen didn't seem to know her finger was on it.

"I thought we'd start with the salads after we feed the kiddos some breakfast. I made a breakfast casserole last night. I know. I cook when I'm nervous. I figured we could use something in the morning anyway," Avery was saying.

"She really does cook when she's nervous. She made two pies last night, too," Serena explained. "The good news is when I'm nervous, I like to clean."

They all had their roles. Avery cooked. Serena cleaned. Charlie tended to play with the kids or organize activities to keep everyone occupied.

"I don't know if I can eat," Serena continued, joining Charlie at the bar. "I got maybe two hours of sleep. I thought we could sentry."

It was what they did. When the mission was long, they got together and took turns napping while the other two watched kids and waited for word.

Ian wanted that song. Guns N' Roses soothed him. It freaking soothed him and let him think better. He needed that stupid song and she couldn't get it to pull up.

What was she doing wrong? He needed this and she was failing. One thing. He'd asked one thing of her and she couldn't manage to do it.

Panic welled. Was the op starting and he didn't have what he needed? What if that stupid song proved the difference in whether he could focus? What if he hesitated because he was waiting on her and she couldn't even work a damn phone app?

"Charlotte?"

She could barely see the fucking screen. "Ian needs a song. I have to get him his song."

It hadn't been so long since they'd gotten Theo back. Her stomach clenched. She'd been standing there beside Ian when he'd gotten the news. She'd watched him pale as the fact that his youngest brother was dead had washed over him. She'd been the one to hold on to him briefly before he'd left to find the body and save the rest of the team.

She'd been there when he'd come home and held her like he would never let her go. Weeks had passed and he'd been stoic and calm in public, and in private he'd spent every moment he could inside her, holding her, letting her be his rock.

Who would be hers if she lost her husband?

She wasn't going to find out because she would figure out how to get him that fucking song.

Serena's hand came out over the phone. "Sweetie, I don't think it works like that. Here, let me try. What do you need to do?"

That was when she noticed her hand was shaking. Charlie took a deep breath. This wasn't the place to break down.

"Charlotte, it's okay." Avery was there, too, her voice warm and steady. "We're all feeling it. It hasn't been too long since Theo died. This is the first real op the guys have been on."

"Ian and Case went to save Theo," she pointed out. Why was she reacting this way? It wasn't the first op. She'd had over a year to get over this. Where was the panic coming from? It welled up along with the frustration at her stupid fucking phone.

Mia Lawless Taggart walked out of the hallway, a baby in her arms. Though Charlie couldn't see it, she knew there was one in her belly, too. Case's first child. Mia bounced the baby wrapped in the pink blanket gently. Brianna, Serena's daughter. "But we didn't know when they would be in danger. That mission took a solid week. It was easier. Way easier. It was kind of like they were on a trip. I don't like this part. I know it's going down any minute and I'm terrified."

Mia was scared? Of course she was. Charlie felt herself center. Mia hadn't been married to Case for long and she was right. When Ian and Case had gone to Europe to look for Hope McDonald, they'd been playing a long game. They'd contacted home every day and it was like they were simply men on a business trip. She and Mia hadn't known until Ian had called and said it was over what was really happening at any point in time.

Charlie put her hands on Mia's shoulders, giving her what she hoped was a reassuring smile. "It's all right, sweetie. This is the gig and we've done it a million times, and every single time, they walk through that door." Yes, this was what she needed. "And they'll be hungry. Ian's always hungry after a killing spree."

Mia's lips curled up slightly. "That's not what Case will want."

Neither would Ian, but some things had to wait a while. "Well, then he shouldn't have picked today for his killing spree. Come on, let's get the kiddos fed and then we'll take some nap sentry duty. It was a long night. It's going to be a longer day. Think of it as our version of girls' night, except it's daytime and no one's getting a stripper. Well, not until the guys come home. I assure you at some point in time they'll all get naked and needy."

"Speaking of girls' night," Avery said, carrying a tray. "A venerable girls' night tradition is drinking. I thought we'd start with Sparkling Screwdrivers. Well, for everyone but the pregnant chicks. Ours is just orange juice. Sorry, sister."

Mia sighed and held Brianna closer. "I miss out on all the fun these days."

"Got it." Serena handed her phone back. "I sent him a playlist of all the best G N' R, starting with 'Welcome to the Jungle'."

A wave of relief swept through her. It would be okay. She took the screwdriver and lifted her glass. "To girls' night."

"And day," Avery said.

They all lifted their glasses and Charlie knew what she was really toasting. "To the sisterhood."

"To the sisterhood," they said solemnly.

To the sisterhood that held them all up and allowed them to break when they needed to. To the sisterhood that gave them understanding and support. It was the same sisterhood that every cop's wife, soldier's honey, or fireman's mother built around herself and her community so they could survive loving someone they could so easily lose.

To the sisterhood she'd found and would fiercely protect. They held each other's hands and babies. They brought food and comfort when needed. They understood.

They clinked glasses and the solemn moment was over.

"Let's turn on some of that sweet Guns N' Roses and get this party started," Charlie said, stronger than she'd been before.

After all, they had work to do, too.

Serena

Serena took a deep breath, trying to think about anything else. She heard the chatter around her, but didn't feel much like talking. Not yet. Her mind wouldn't stop though. Her mind just kept whirling and coming back to the bad stuff.

Work. She would think about work. Work was always good.

Start at the beginning.

Chapter One

Mila looked across the room and saw the amazingly hot man. Who was he? Where had he come from? Why was he wearing skinny jeans?

Nope. Serena discarded that line of thinking at the same time she tossed out the egg shells. She started to whisk those eggs as she tried to concentrate. No skinny jeans. No matter what Adam thought, skinny jeans shouldn't be on one of her heroes. And some men could totally rock a pink polo, but Adam wasn't one of them. She'd kept her mouth closed when she'd caught Jake throwing it out.

Was Adam alone? How long had he been in position? She worried about him during a mission like this. Was he scared?

Nope. Jake was there. They would take care of each other.

Was Avery going to make more screwdrivers? Sometimes the pregnant chicks didn't remember that alcohol totally helped.

She looked at the oven and raised the temp to 425. They had to feed the babies.

Maybe she should write another small town book. It had been a long time. She'd gotten caught up in the romantic suspense. Sometimes it was good to change things up.

She would run it by her writer friends group. She was due to go to a retreat in Colorado in a few weeks. Creede, Colorado.

Should she go? With everything happening at home, maybe she should skip it.

Although Colorado was beautiful. Maybe she needed some inspiration. A couple of hot Colorado cowboys. They would be on horseback when the heroine first saw them and then…oh, then she would turn and her breath would be taken away…

"Serena?"

She glanced up. Charlotte was staring at her. "Did you hear a word I said?"

She smiled. It was the best way to get through it. That and lying. She wasn't capable of concentrating on a day like today. "Sure."

Charlotte went on about how pissed she was at her Internet music provider and Serena let her mind wander.

Or she could write about a Texas town. Yeah, she might be going about this wrong. She wrote about a lot of small towns where ménage was the norm. But what about a Texas town where it wasn't, where the heroine would have to fight small minds to catch her hot cowboys.

It could start with a woman coming home after being run out of town twenty years before…

Mia

Mia glanced at the clock. Not even noon. Her phone, unlike Charlotte's, had been radio silent. Apparently her husband didn't need a "theme song," unlike his big brother.

"You okay?" Avery asked. She was standing in the kitchen, peeling potatoes while Charlotte cleaned up after breakfast.

Mia was simply trying to take it all in. Breakfast with eight kiddos under the age of five was a truly eye-opening experience. She almost might be wondering what the hell she was doing thinking she could handle a family like this.

Charlotte kept everything moving smoothly. She was the boss and nothing fazed her. Serena seemed to be working on something. She kept making notes on plots and characters. Avery was peaceful and calm, her tone soothing.

Mia felt like a fucking wreck.

Her stomach churned and the toast she'd managed to down threatened to come back up. "I'm fine."

Deep breath. Oh, this baby boy was going to kill her. When she looked in the mirror, she could see only the faintest hint of a curve to her stomach, but her son was making himself felt.

Charlotte looked up, shaking her head. "She's green. I think we should call a code seven up on that one."

Ah, the sarcasm of her inlaws. A code seven up meant someone was about to blow, usually either a kid or a pregnant woman, though she'd seen one called on Adam when he'd changed a particularly nasty diaper once. She was going to have one of those wriggling, needy things, and she would be the one here waiting to find out if her husband had made it while she took care of their son.

It was so unfair.

Another deep breath. She was stuck at home while Case wandered the world, while Case put himself in perpetual danger for a job he didn't need because she had the means to provide for them all. He was out there right now waiting to get his hot ass killed, and why?

They had millions of dollars at their fingertips. They had a private jet. Of course it was all courtesy of her brother, but it was still right there.

"Nope," Avery said, taking her hand. "Let's go. Even if you don't need to throw up, you need something. You're going from red to green to sheet white."

She'd lost her parents when she was six years old. Would this baby of hers lose Daddy before he even got out of the womb? Was her family cursed?

Avery gently started to pull her into the hallway. Then she didn't have to because Mia realized that nothing was going to stop what was happening in her gut. She sprinted toward the bathroom and barely managed to make it there before breakfast took an encore.

"Yep, I hated this part," Avery was saying as she knelt down and held Mia's hair.

All her life she'd wanted sisters. Now they seemed to be everywhere. Magnificent women who tried to take care of her. If it hadn't been Avery it would have been Serena or Charlotte. When she was home, Ellie or Carly or Shelby took on the duty. Case tried, but then he got sympathy nausea and she usually ended up taking care of him.

Men.

She forced herself to stand and wash her mouth out.

Mia sank back down to the floor, her body weak. "Sorry. I made it through the first couple of months with no problems at all, but the last few weeks have been hell on my stomach."

Avery sat with her, both their backs to Serena's big tub. "I knew I was pregnant with Aidan when I woke up one morning and couldn't get to the bathroom fast enough. I think this one might be a girl. I had to take a test to be sure I was expecting. The only sign was missing my period. She's perfectly well behaved. Not a single incidence of morning sickness. Also, morning sickness is a misnomer. It can happen any time."

"It sucks."

"It also gets better," Avery assured her. "You'll hit this magical time when the sickness goes away and you'll feel good again, and if you're lucky you'll feel very, very sexy."

Mia had to laugh. "I think I already have that part down. When I'm not tired or sick, I'm super horny. It's been a fun, unexpected twist to the pregnancy thing."

Sometimes her husband walked in the room and she jumped him. She couldn't help it. She needed him inside her. It was kind of awesome.

"Ah, hormones. Enjoy it now because they bite you in the butt in the end." Avery passed her a can of green cold goodness.

She took a long drink. That was so much better. "Do you ever get used to this?"

"To what? Pregnancy, or the sitting at home and waiting to see if your man gets shot thing?"

Tears pierced Mia's eyes as the memory surfaced as clear and cutting as though it had happened yesterday. When she closed her eyes, she could still see Case falling, see the blood bloom on his chest and feel the horror of being dragged away from him. "I watched Case get shot once. I don't know what's worse—seeing it or worrying about it when I can't see it."

Avery sighed. "I think watching it is definitely worse. I was there when Eli Nelson shot Li. It was only a couple of times, but in my mind it was a hundred. Li covered me. He took bullet after bullet for me, and then Nelson was nice enough to give us a head start before he blew up the house we were in. I had to drag Li out because he couldn't move."

"I remember how hard it was to watch Case going after Theo. He couldn't shoot his brother, but Theo didn't know who he was. It was awful. I was there and I wished that if someone died, it would be me. And that was a completely selfish thought."

"Because you didn't want to be the one left behind," Avery said. "Believe me, I know that thought well. We've all had it. To answer your question more thoroughly, it does get easier because you learn to trust him. You figure out that he's not as reckless as he was when he was a kid. Li knows his time in the field is coming to an end. I think he's looking forward to today because soon he'll have two kids, and with half the team forming their own thing, he's going to have to take on some administrative duties."

Adam, Jake, and Si, Jesse, and their wives would be on their own soon. Big Tag would bring in new operatives, young men and women without families who would take over for the older operatives in the field. No one wanted to be away from their kiddos for too long. It was the way their world worked. How would Case handle it when the inevitable time came?

"Does that make him mad? I ask because I think it would upset Case if he had to be behind a desk."

Avery shook her head. "No. He knows that Adam is far too brilliant to stay where he is forever. He's always known that. Adam and Chelsea are going to bring peace to a lot of people. And it's natural for their partners and spouses to go with them. And it's natural that Ian, Alex, and Li take on more managerial roles. Does it make you mad?"

She shook her head. McKay-Taggart had always felt like a family to her. It must hurt to break a big piece of it off, but she understood ambition. "Of course not. I think what they're doing is amazing. They're going to find missing people. I'm excited about it. Adam said I could follow him around, maybe write a story about the company as they try to figure out who the Lost Boys are."

"I meant does it make you mad that you have to be the one who sits behind a desk now?"

She turned to Avery, who had so precisely stated her feelings. "I can't risk our baby."

"But it hurts you the same way it hurts Charlotte. Like Serena said, she and I aren't warriors. I always knew I wanted to stay home and raise some kids with a nice man I met. I never imagined I would meet Li and then Serena and that we would build a business of our own, but it's not as exciting as going around the world and reporting on war zones."

She'd loved her job. Her job had taken her to some of the craziest places in the world, some of the most dangerous places, too. "I lost my mom and dad at a young age. I can't risk losing this baby. I can't risk him losing one of us."

"Are you mad at Case for still putting himself out there? It's okay if you are. Love is a complex thing, but sometimes admitting our feelings helps us get over them."

She thought about it for a moment, finally examining her feelings. What was she? Worried. A little sad that part of her life was mostly over. Was she angry?

Life was a set of choices. Case would have been happy to split his time. Before she'd gotten pregnant, he followed her when she wanted to write a story. He'd helped with her brothers and never complained.

Tears started to fall. "Case wouldn't be Case if he didn't work."

Did she want Case to take some corporate job with her brother's company where he would always be safe and the worst he would deal with was running employee background checks? It wasn't about the money for Case. It was about who he was.

She hadn't fallen for him because he was safe. She certainly hadn't fallen for him because he wanted to sit around and be idly wealthy. That wasn't Case at all.

"I like writing fiction," she admitted. "It's a much easier transition for me than him. It's not because I'm the woman. I'm sure for some couples it is, but not us. Case was happy to follow me around the world and make sure I stay safe."

"But you're having a baby and he needs roots. One of you has to come home," Avery said gently.

"Me. I'm going to do it." Somehow saying it out loud made her feel better. "You know I was raised by my moms."

Avery grinned. "I love your moms. They make the best chili."

Mia wiped her eyes. "Mama does. And then Mom was a doctor. She worked in a trauma unit and kept crazy hours. Mama wanted to own a bakery. Then I came along and they decided someone needed to be there for me. I was a…how do I put it…needy wreck when I got to their house."

She'd been in foster care for a couple of months when she'd landed with her moms. She'd shown up with all of her meager possessions in a garbage bag, and she hadn't unpacked for three weeks.

"You had been through a lot," Avery said quietly.

"Mama had saved up money to start her business. She had this place in Deep Ellum picked out, and then she realized I would have to go into after-school care, potentially before-school care because bakeries open early for breakfast. That is perfectly fine for some kids."

"But you desperately needed the stability of a stay-at-home parent after all that chaos," Avery concluded.

The memories came back to her, easing her and making her tear up at the same time. Despite everything, she'd been loved. There was no such thing as having it all. There was love and joy and sacrifice. There were decisions to be made for the betterment of the whole family. "So she changed her dreams and worked from home. I got to help. I still love to bake. It's soothing to me. It makes me feel loved. I'm going to give that to my kids. Life is a set of choices and I think I just came to terms with mine."

And when she thought about it, she didn't totally have to choose. There would still be research trips. She would need to see and visit the places she wrote about. She would simply have to be more careful about it because her life would be precious to her child. Precious to her husband, too. What had it taken for Case to let her go those six months before she'd listened to his voicemails? He'd loved her and he'd given her the time and space she'd needed. He'd kept his hands off even as he'd known she'd been in danger.

"I think I want to make a chocolate cake," she said suddenly. Like most times during this part of her pregnancy, mornings of nausea were lifted by afternoons filled with energy and light.

Avery got to her feet and held out a hand. "I think we can manage that."

Case would be hungry when he came home. Hungry for everything, and she intended to give it to him.

Serena

Should she have the alpha male shoot the villain? Maybe that was way too obvious. She needed a twist. God, she shot a lot of people. In a fictional way.

Jake got shot. In a real way. Adam had scars all over his body that spoke of how often he'd danced with the reaper.

Nope. Not going there. She had a book to plot. Didn't she always?

A good twisty murder mystery.

That was what would get everyone's minds off the fact that there were not only Ukrainian assholes after her hot hubbies, but also a bunch of Dutch mercenaries. Everyone was trying to kill her men.

Serena stared at the ceiling. It was her nap time. How was she supposed to sleep? Despite the fact that she'd been awake for over twenty-four hours, her freaking brain wouldn't turn off. How was she supposed to turn it off without fifty orgasms? When Adam and Jake were here they would just fuck her calm. She was totally good with that plan.

She closed her eyes. Only one more hour. She needed sleep or she would be a zombie and it was Jake's birthday.

Maybe not so twisty a story. Maybe this story would be predictable and routine and the bad guys would be defeated with ease. Yes. That was the story she wanted today.

Sleep. She needed an hour of sleep and she would be able to deal.

How many characters had she written whose names started with A?

Aaron. Amelia. Annie.

She started to count characters and briefly managed some sleep.

Avery

She wasn't sure how Serena could sleep. Probably because she had two men and knew they would watch after each other.

No. That wasn't fair. Jake and Adam were as much on the line as anyone else. They didn't merely watch after each other. They would be in the middle of the fight, watching after Li and the rest.

They were all one big family.

She had to hold on to that thought.

Because she couldn't lose another husband. She couldn't go through that again. No. The universe couldn't possibly be that cruel.

What time was it? Almost two in the afternoon. The kids were napping. Serena was down for the count. They'd made all the pies and cakes. Most of the sides. The meat was marinating and she was standing out here in the heat of the afternoon prepping for a party that might or might not happen.

That would happen.

"You need help with that?" Grace stepped outside and took the other end of the tablecloth, helping her spread it over the long picnic table. "Sorry we're late. Lucas had an ear infection. He's fine this morning, but it was a hell of a night. Not that we're the only ones who had a bad night. Have you heard anything?"

She shook her head. Sometimes she thought Grace had gotten the best deal of the lot of them. Sean's passion was food. Still, of all the women here, Grace was the one who understood what loss truly meant. She'd lost a husband, too. "Not a word. I'm sure they're fine."

Grace's eyes widened. "Oh, this is the moment when I would grab a bottle of wine, if you could. Avery, it's all right to be upset. You know if you don't talk about it, it festers and causes trouble down the road."

Sometimes it was like standing in front of a crowd and introducing yourself. *Hello, I'm Avery and I'm a one-time widow, shooting to not lose husband number two and worried that I will because the way I feel about him totally eclipses anything I felt for the first one. Because sometimes, deep down, I'm okay with how things went because I love him and our life together so, so much I can barely stand it.*

How could she think that? How could she expect to think that way and not have something terrible happen?

This was the worst time. Everything was quiet. This was when she couldn't stop her brain from working overtime. She would find something to do. They would call any minute now. Or they would decide to play a little trick on the women and simply walk right through the door. Li would walk in any moment.

She smoothed the tablecloth down, trying to make it as perfect as possible.

Grace reached out, putting a hand over hers. "Avery, it's okay to freak out and you know it. You're the one who always says if one of us doesn't have a breakdown, it's not an op."

Because this was their op. This was their trial. Waiting. Keeping the home fires burning.

"I can't stop thinking about what happened to Brandon and Maddie." Her hands were shaking. So many years had passed and yet sometimes the pain was fresh and slicing.

"Of course you can't." Charlotte stepped through the patio door and out into the backyard. "Stephanie's here. She's also in danger, and everything you sacrificed for is up in the air. Avery, I can't believe you're standing upright."

It so sucked that she couldn't down a bottle of wine and numb herself while this was going on. Steph was out there somewhere with a gun pointed at her head. Li was trying to save her. She could lose them all.

She looked to Grace. "When is it okay to be okay with it?"

Grace's eyes went soft and understanding. She stepped in and put her hands on Avery's shoulders. "It's all right. It's okay now. I think the same things and guilt threatens to overwhelm me, but I also know that it's all right to be happy things turned out the way they did."

Charlotte joined them. "What are you talking about?"

Serena and Mia stepped outside.

"Is everything all right?" Serena asked, yawning.

Suddenly nothing at all seemed right. It had been too long. They'd heard nothing. Absolutely nothing. Her phone had been completely silent. What if someone died? She knew what team protocol was. They would go silent until the family could be notified. There would be no cheery texts saying they would be home soon. There would be silence.

She couldn't do it again. She couldn't lose Li.

"I wouldn't change anything." Avery admitted her guilt. "I would go through it all again if it meant being right here. What kind of person does that make me?"

They moved around her, forming a circle, surrounding her.

"Oh, Avery, it makes you human and happy," Charlotte said.

Grace looked down at her. "We can't go back and change the past. We can only move forward. I know my husband would be happy for me. He would be happy for our boys, that they got a kick-ass stepfather to help them through adulthood. He would be happy that I found someone who loves me like no one else in the world. Avery, we can't help that we're happy and they're gone. We can only thank the universe for sending us something to ease the ache of losing them."

"I think about the fact that if my mom had lived, if I hadn't been kidnapped by my dad, I would be an entirely different person. I wouldn't be Ian's Charlie," Charlotte said solemnly. "I've known some of the lowest lows a person can know in the world, but I made the choice to also accept the highs. I wouldn't go back. This is my life and I'll take every minute of it."

The goods. The bads. The long waits in between. All of it worthwhile. All of it precious.

They held on to each other, the circle closing around Avery. A silence descended and she knew what every woman was thinking.

Bring him home to me. Safe and sound. Let this be a good day. But if it's not a good day, if it's the day we all dread, then thank you for the women who surround me. Thank you for the sisterhood that lifts me up and reminds me I am never alone.

A single cell phone pinged, breaking their silent communion.

And then another. And another.

And Avery felt hers go off.

She pulled it from her jeans pocket.

All safe and sound, love. Though it looks like Brody's got his knickers in a terrible twist. We've got some cupid work to do. Get that food ready because you've got a hungry lot coming your way. I love you, me darlin'.

She breathed for the first time in hours.

Not today. It wouldn't be today.

Charlotte's head fell back on a happy groan. "Thank god. Girls, let's get this party started. Who wants tequila?"

Mia raised her hand. "I want it. I want it so bad. I'll settle for ice cream."

Grace wrapped an arm around Charlotte's waist. "Come on, sister. I've got Sean already cutting up limes for us."

Serena smiled as the others filed in. "I'll get the grill started. Damn. I told Jake to move it. There are bees in those bushes."

Avery smiled and took a moment to let the sun warm her face. There were times when she was truly happy to be alive and loved. They were coming home. For some families, the idea that they could be torn apart never occurred to them except in an abstract fashion. But she was aware every day. That meant she had to be grateful every single day.

Thankful for another moment, another day, another week and month and year with him.

With her family.

"Don't worry about it," she told Serena. "They just dodged a thousand bullets. A few bees can't do much harm. Let's get the salads ready."

Serena joined her. Their men were coming home.

It was time to celebrate.

Index

RECIPES

Appetizers and Sides

Bacon Ranch Cheese Ball	5
Bacon Wrapped Shrimp	2
Cheesy Monkey Bread	47
Coconut Shrimp	4
Hot Ham & Cheese Rolls	128
Meatball Sliders	48
Slow Cooker Spinach & Artichoke Dip	46
Stuffed Mushrooms	3
Texas Caviar	82
Wild Rice Dressing with Sausage & Cranberries	129

Main Dishes

Beef Wellington	6
Burrito Love	84
Sausage Ravioli Alfredo	49
Slow Cooker Beef and Broccoli	19
Slow Cooker Cheeseburger Meatloaf	86
Slow Cooker Chicken & Dumplings	130
Slow Cooker Chili	95
Slow Cooker Honey Soy Pot Roast	131
Slow Cooker Pizza Chicken	61
Slow Cooker Pork Tenderloin with Pineapple	18
Slow Cooker Stuffed Bell Peppers	60
Southwest Chicken	85
Taco Ring of Fire	83

Salads

Artichoke Salad 62
Strawberry Pretzel Salad 21

Breakfast

Easy Breakfast Casserole 132
Stuffed French Toast 96

Desserts

Apple Turnovers 97
Banana Pudding 145
Chocolate Cake with Chocolate Icing 20
Easy Tiramisu 63
Ice Cream Cake 98
Key Lime Cake 147
Peach Cobbler 146

Drinks

Blackberry Moscow Mule 99
Sparkling Screwdriver 22
Spiked Strawberry Lemonade 148

SLICES OF LIFE AND SHORT STORIES

CHARLOTTE
Slice of Life - Phoebe and Jesse in "Mischief Managed" 7
Charlotte and Ian's story - Rough Night 23

FAITH
Slice of Life - Karina and Derek in "Stakeout Takeout" 50
Faith and Ten's story - Unexpected Gifts 64

SERENA
Slice of Life - Tiffany and Sebastian in "After Hours" 87
Serena's story - Broke Down in Bliss 100

PENNY
Slice of Life - Damon and Penny in "She's the Boss" 133
Women of McKay-Taggart - The Long Wait 149

Other Books by Lexi Blake

EROTIC ROMANCE

MASTERS AND MERCENARIES

The Dom Who Loved Me
The Men With The Golden Cuffs
A Dom is Forever
On Her Master's Secret Service
Sanctum: A Masters and Mercenaries Novella
Love and Let Die
Unconditional: A Masters and Mercenaries Novella
Dungeon Royale
Dungeon Games: A Masters and Mercenaries Novella
A View to a Thrill
Cherished: A Masters and Mercenaries Novella
You Only Love Twice
Luscious: Masters and Mercenaries~Topped
Adored: A Masters and Mercenaries Novella
Master No
Just One Taste: Masters and Mercenaries~Topped 2
From Sanctum with Love
Devoted: A Masters and Mercenaries Novella
Dominance Never Dies
Submission is Not Enough

Masters and Mercenaries, continued

Master Bits and Mercenary Bites~The Secret Recipes of Topped

Perfectly Paired: Masters and Mercenaries~Topped 3

For His Eyes Only

Arranged: A Masters and Mercenaries Novella

Love Another Day

At Your Service: Masters and Mercenaries~Topped 4

Nobody Does It Better, Coming February 20, 2018

Close Cover, Coming April 10, 2018

Protected, Coming July 31, 2018

Lawless

Ruthless

Satisfaction

Revenge

Courting Justice

Order of Protection, Coming June 5, 2018

Masters Of Ménage
(by Shayla Black and Lexi Blake)

Their Virgin Captive

Their Virgin's Secret

Their Virgin Concubine

Their Virgin Princess

Their Virgin Hostage

Their Virgin Secretary

Their Virgin Mistress

The Perfect Gentlemen
(by Shayla Black and Lexi Blake)

Scandal Never Sleeps

Seduction in Session

Big Easy Temptation

Smoke and Sin

At the Pleasure of the President, Coming Fall 2018

URBAN FANTASY

Thieves

Steal the Light

Steal the Day

Steal the Moon

Steal the Sun

Steal the Night

Ripper

Addict

Sleeper

Outcast, Coming 2018

LEXI BLAKE WRITING AS SOPHIE OAK

Texas Sirens

Small Town Siren, Coming January 9, 2018

Other Books by Suzanne McCollum Johnson

Southern Bits & Bites

Southern Kid Bits & Mom Bites

Southern Bits & Bites: Our 150 Favorite Recipes

Writing with Lexi Blake

Master Bits & Mercenary Bites

Writing with J. Kenner

Bar Bites: A Man of the Month Cookbook